Higher

Physical Education

2005 SQP
_____

2005 Exam
_____

2006 Exam
_____

2007 Exam
_____

2008 Exam
_____

Leckie × Leckie

First exam published in 2005.

Published by Leckie & Leckie Ltd, 3rd Floor, 4 Queen Street, Edinburgh EH2 1JE

tel: 0131 220 6831 fax: 0131 225 9987 enquiries@leckieandleckie.co.uk www.leckieandleckie.co.uk

ISBN 978-1-84372-685-2

A CIP Catalogue record for this book is available from the British Library.

Leckie & Leckie is a division of Huveaux plc.

Leckie & Leckie is grateful to the copyright holders, as credited at the back of the book, for permission to use their material.
Every effort has been made to trace the copyright holders and to obtain their permission for the use of copyright material.
Leckie & Leckie will gladly receive information enabling them to rectify any error or omission in subsequent editions.

Dear Student

In 2005 the format of the Higher Physical Education exam was changed. The following Specimen Question Paper and actual exams will give you good practice in the new format.

Here is some information about the new exam format:

The Question Paper
- You can score up to 60 marks.

- You will be allowed 2 hours 30 minutes for this exam.

- It will test your ability to understand and apply your skills and Key Concept knowledge of Analysis and Development of Performance and each Area of Analysis.

- It will be in four sections, one per Area of Analysis

- You will have to answer three questions in total, each chosen from a different section. Within each section there are two questions.

Each question will:
- be worth 20 marks and will be split into four parts

- will be answerable by all candidates in that it will not be specific to any particular activity

- have links between its parts, testing your relevant Key Concepts knowledge and analysis skills

- ask you to use your relevant practical experiences.

In answering the questions, you will need to show your abilities to:
- describe, record and clearly explain features of your performance

- use a range of relevant concepts and knowledge to analyse performance

- apply knowledge and understanding when discussing the design, completion and monitoring of programmes of work that are likely to lead to performance development

- complete an evaluation of the analysis and development process.

Please visit *www.sqa.org.uk* for further details.

[BLANK PAGE]

[C205/SQP233]

Physical Education   Time: 2 hours 30 mins   NATIONAL
Higher   QUALIFICATIONS
Specimen Question Paper
for use in and after 2005

Candidates should attempt **three** questions, **each** chosen from a **different section**.

SCOTTISH
QUALIFICATIONS
AUTHORITY

SECTION 1: PERFORMANCE APPRECIATION

Marks

Question 1

Choose **one** activity.

(a) Discuss, both, the **challenges** of this activity for you and the **qualities** you identified as your strengths and development needs.

6

(b) Choose **one** of the **qualities** discussed in Part (a) that was identified as a **development need**.

Describe the extent of the development need and exactly how it was identified.

4

(c) **Awareness of performance weaknesses can be distracting during performance**.

Discuss this statement with reference to the management of your performance and with reference to how model performers manage these situations.

6

(d) Discuss how you can plan and manage your performance improvement in the short and/or longer term.

4

(20)

Question 2

Choose **one** activity.

(a) During your course you will have gathered data about **different aspects** of your **whole performance** in this activity. Discuss the significance of the information your data generated for **two** different aspects of your performance.

6

(b) Discuss how you used this information to develop a training programme to meet your identified training needs. For **each** aspect of your performance give specific examples of what you did.

6

(c) Describe how you managed your training **over a period of time** and explain any **changes** you made to your programme.

4

(d) Describe **how** your training influenced your ability to meet the **demands** of performance in your chosen activity.

4

(20)

SECTION 2: PREPARATION OF THE BODY

Marks

Question 3

Choose **an** activity.

(*a*) Describe the **methods** you used to assess your fitness to meet the demands of performance in this activity.   **4**

(*b*) Use your knowledge and understanding to explain the **principles** that underpin **progressive fitness training**.   **4**

(*c*) Discuss **one method** of training you used and the **advantages** it offered for developing a **specific type** of fitness for performance in this activity.   **6**

(*d*) Discuss how you applied the principles of training identified in Part (*b*) in planning and carrying out the training method you used. Support your discussion with specific examples from your training programme.   **6**

(20)

Question 4

Choose **an** activity.

(*a*) Use your knowledge and understanding to discuss why **one aspect of each** of the following **types of fitness** is needed for successful performance in the chosen activity.

- **physical fitness**
- **skill-related fitness**
- **mental fitness**   **6**

(*b*) Choose **one** of the **aspects** of fitness you identified in Part (*a*). Discuss your knowledge of **fitness assessment methods** in relation to this aspect of fitness and the information different methods can provide.   **4**

(*c*) Describe, in detail, the content of a **training programme** where you focused on the **aspect of fitness** identified in Part (*b*) to develop your performance.   **6**

(*d*) Choose **one** of the other **aspects of fitness** you identified in Part (*a*). For this aspect discuss your future training needs to further develop your performance.   **4**

(20)

SECTION 3: SKILLS AND TECHNIQUES

Marks

Question 5

Choose **one** activity.

(*a*)   Describe some of the features of performance that can be identified at each of the **stages of skill learning**.   Give specific examples from the chosen activity.

6

(*b*)   Select a skill or technique from your activity.   Give a **detailed analysis** of the features of **your** performance that clearly mark out your **current** stage of learning.

4

(*c*)   When developing this skill or technique discuss how you used your knowledge of skill learning to design an appropriate programme of work. Give specific details of the programme you used.

6

(*d*)   Describe how you evaluated the effectiveness of the programme you used.

4

(20)

Question 6

(*a*)   Explain, in detail, what you understand about **information processing** and its relevance to learning and developing skill or refining technique.

6

(*b*)   Select a complex skill or technique from an activity of your choice.   When developing **or** refining **or** applying this skill or technique, discuss the **range of information** you had to process to ensure your performance improved.

4

(*c*)   Describe, in detail, the **methods of practice** you used to improve your ability in the chosen skill or technique with a view to improving your whole performance.

6

(*d*)   Describe, in detail, how you monitored your progress during practice. Explain what you did to ensure your progress was continuous.

4

(20)

SECTION 4: STRUCTURES, STRATEGIES AND COMPOSITION

Marks

Question 7

(a) Choose an activity and a structure, strategy or composition you have used. Describe how you **planned your practice** of this structure, strategy or composition to ensure you were prepared to **apply and adapt** it as performance circumstances required.

6

(b) When using this structure, strategy or composition describe how your strength(s) and weakness(es) influenced your practice and performance.

4

(c) Discuss how you **adapted your performance** in this structure, strategy or composition to reduce the effect of your weakness(es). Explain, in detail, the adaptations you made to minimize identified weakness(es).

6

(d) As a result of the adaptations you made, describe how you evaluated the effectiveness of the performance. Identify **one** future development need within this structure, strategy or composition.

4

(20)

Question 8

(a) Describe, in detail, a structure, strategy or composition that you would usually select as your **first choice**. Explain why you would select this structure, strategy or composition in preference to any other.

6

(b) Discuss the importance of developing **alternative** structures, strategies or compositions when practicing to meet **less predictable** performance demands.

6

(c) **During the application of a structure, strategy or composition focusing your attention on relevant information can ensure that effective decisions are made.**

With reference to the role you played **or** a performance you planned give examples of **two pieces of information** you would look for to help inform your decision making.

4

(d) Discuss how you would organise your future training to ensure you had **opportunities to practice decision-making** when applying structures, strategies or compositions.

4

(20)

[END OF SPECIMEN QUESTION PAPER]

[BLANK PAGE]

[BLANK PAGE]

X205/301

NATIONAL
QUALIFICATIONS
2005

THURSDAY, 2 JUNE
1.00 PM – 3.30 PM

PHYSICAL
EDUCATION
HIGHER
Analysis and
Development of
Performance

Candidates should attempt **three** questions, each chosen from a different area.

SCOTTISH
QUALIFICATIONS
AUTHORITY

AREA 1: PERFORMANCE APPRECIATION

Marks

Question 1

Choose an activity.

(*a*) Discuss the **qualities** that you consider to be **strengths** in your performance.   **4**

(*b*) Describe how you planned to improve **two different areas** of your performance in this activity over a specified period of time.   **6**

(*c*) Describe how you monitored your progress during training. Explain the impact the training had on your **whole** performance.   **6**

(*d*) Discuss how you used **models** of performance to evaluate the development of **your** performance.   **4**

    (20)

Question 2

Choose an activity.

(*a*) Describe how you obtained data about **two different areas** of your whole performance. What information about **specific development needs** did your data provide?   **6**

(*b*) Outline the training programme you planned to meet your development needs.   **4**

(*c*) **Justify** the relevance of the training you planned. Explain any adaptations you made over a period of time.   **5**

(*d*) Discuss the value of **setting goals** when planning training to develop your performance.   **5**

    (20)

AREA 2: PREPARATION OF THE BODY

Marks

Question 3

Choose an activity.

(a) **Physical, skill-related** and **mental fitness** are all required for successful performance. With reference to your chosen activity, explain why **one aspect** of **each** of these **types of fitness** is important.   6

(b) Choose **two** different **methods of training** that you have used (or have considered using) to develop **one** of the types of fitness discussed in part (*a*).

Discuss the merits that **each** method offers for the development of your performance in your chosen activity.   5

(c) With specific reference to **one** method of training discussed in part (*b*), explain the importance of **progressively overloading** your training. Give specific examples.   5

(d) Discuss the effects that your training had on your **whole performance**.   4

(20)

Question 4

Choose an activity.

(a) Discuss why it is important to ensure that fitness training is:

   (i) specific to the **fitness demands of the activity**; and

   (ii) specific to the **personal needs** of the performer.   6

(b) With reference to the specific demands of the activity, describe the **methods used** to make observations, and record data, about your fitness for performance. Briefly describe the development **needs** that you identified.   6

(c) Outline a programme of work you used to meet the needs you identified.   4

(d) With reference to your **whole performance**, discuss the effectiveness of your programme of work.   4

(20)

[Turn over

AREA 3: SKILLS AND TECHNIQUES

Marks

Question 5

Choose an activity.

(a) Explain in detail, what you understand about the **principles of effective practice** when developing skill and/or refining technique.   5

(b) Select a skill or technique. Discuss **how you used** data gathered, and other information sources, to plan your performance development.   5

(c) Describe, in detail, a **programme of work** you used to develop this skill or technique. Give examples of how the **principles of effective practice** were applied in the programme.   6

(d) On completion of your programme, describe how your **whole performance** was affected. Outline what you would do to ensure your progress continued.   4

(20)

Question 6

Choose an activity and a skill or technique.

(a) What information about your performance were you able to obtain using one of the following **methods of analysis**?

  (i) Mechanical analysis

  (ii) Movement analysis

  (iii) Consideration of quality   4

(b) Describe, in detail, two different **methods of practice** you used to develop your performance of the skill or technique identified. Explain why you considered each of the practice methods selected to be appropriate.   6

(c) From the list below, select **two** of the factors that are **influential** in skill development. Discuss how **each** of the factors chosen affected the development of your skill or technique during practice.

- **Motivation**
- **Feedback**
- **Anxiety**
- **Concentration**
- **Confidence**   6

(d) **"Skilled performers are able to select and apply the right skill at the right time."**

With reference to a **skilled** performance in an activity of your choice, discuss this statement.   4

(20)

AREA 4: STRUCTURES, STRATEGIES AND COMPOSITION   *Marks*

Question 7

Choose an activity.

(*a*) Explain why it is important to consider the demands of the performance situation **before selecting** a Structure, Strategy or Composition. Make reference to the factors you would consider.   **6**

(*b*) Describe, in detail, a Structure, Strategy or Composition that took into account at least **one of the factors** considered in part (*a*).   **4**

(*c*) Describe circumstances that required you to **adapt or change** this Structure, Strategy or Composition. Outline the adaptations or changes you made, and explain how they ensured your performance remained effective.   **6**

(*d*) Describe what you would do in the **longer term** to further improve your ability within the **original** Structure, Strategy or Composition.   **4**

                    (20)

Question 8

Choose an activity.

(*a*) Select a Structure, Strategy or Composition. Describe the **strengths** a performer(s) requires to apply this Structure, Strategy or Composition effectively. For example, you may wish to consider the physical, technical and/or the mental strengths required.   **6**

(*b*) When performing **in the activity chosen**, explain the importance of one of the following factors.

- **Group and team principles**
- **Choreography and composition**
- **Tactical and design elements**   **6**

(*c*) With reference to **the Structure, Strategy or Composition selected** in part (*a*), give specific examples of how the factor described in part (*b*) is applied to ensure an effective performance.   **4**

(*d*) Describe a practice/practice session where you tried to develop your performance **using the factor chosen in part (*b*)**.   **4**

                    (20)

[END OF QUESTION PAPER]

[BLANK PAGE]

[BLANK PAGE]

X205/301

NATIONAL QUALIFICATIONS 2006	WEDNESDAY, 24 MAY 9.00 AM – 11.30 AM	PHYSICAL EDUCATION HIGHER

Candidates should attempt **three** questions, each chosen from a different area.

SCOTTISH
QUALIFICATIONS
AUTHORITY
©

AREA 1: PERFORMANCE APPRECIATION

Marks

Question 1

Choose an activity.

(a) Describe in detail the **range of qualities** you require to perform effectively in your chosen activity.

4

(b) Discuss how **two** of these qualities described in part (a) affected your own performance.

6

(c) Discuss the importance of using **long** and **short** term goals. Give examples of the goals you set to improve your performance.

6

(d) How did you monitor your performance as you worked towards achieving your goals?

4

(20)

Question 2

Choose an activity.

(a) Explain how **mental factors** can influence performance.

4

(b) **Model** performers can cope well with the demands of performance. With reference to **one specific** demand, compare your performance to that of the model performer.

4

(c) Discuss the course of action you would take to bring about an improvement in your performance.

6

(d) Discuss the effectiveness of your course of action. Describe how your overall performance was influenced.

6

(20)

AREA 2: PREPARATION OF THE BODY

Marks

Question 3

Choose an activity.

(a) Describe in detail **one** method you used to assess your fitness in the chosen activity. Explain why this method was appropriate. 4

(b) Select **one** method of training and explain why this method was appropriate. Describe in detail **one** training session using this method. 6

(c) Discuss why the **principles of training** are important when designing a training programme. 6

(d) Explain why it is important to evaluate the effects of your programme on your **overall performance**. 4

(20)

Question 4

Choose an activity.

(a) Describe the fitness requirements needed to perform effectively in the chosen activity. 4

(b) The training year can be divided into **3 phases** or **periods**.

- **Preparation** or **pre-season**
- **Competition** or **in season**
- **Transition** or **off season**

Select **one** phase or period. Describe in detail the content of a training programme you used to develop a **specific type of fitness** during this phase or period. 6

(c) Discuss the importance of planning to help implement and manage your training programme. 6

(d) Discuss the effectiveness of your training programme on your overall performance. Give examples of your future development needs. 4

(20)

[Turn over

AREA 3: SKILLS AND TECHNIQUES

Marks

Question 5

Choose an activity and a skill or technique.

(a) Explain the benefits of considering a model/skilled performance when learning or developing **this** skill or technique.

4

(b) Describe, briefly, how you gathered data/information about your performance in this selected skill or technique. Give specific details of how your performance **compared** to that of a model/skilled performance.

6

(c) In relation to your current performance, describe in detail a programme of work that would be appropriate to develop the skill or technique identified.

6

(d) Explain why it is important to monitor the effectiveness of your programme of work.

4

(20)

Question 6

(a) From your experience in one activity, describe a **complex** skill or technique you have attempted to develop. Explain why you found this skill or technique difficult to perform.

4

(b) Describe, in detail, **two** methods of practice you used and considered important to develop this skill or technique.

6

(c) Explain, in detail, the **principles** you took into account when using these methods of practice to ensure your programme was effective.

6

(d) Having developed your skill or technique in practice, discuss why your performance may still not be effective when applying **this** skill or technique during **whole** performance.

4

(20)

AREA 4: STRUCTURES, STRATEGIES AND COMPOSITION

Marks

Question 7

Choose an activity.

(a) Describe, in detail, a Structure, Strategy or Composition you have used. Outline the **role** you performed when applying this Structure, Strategy or Composition.

6

(b) When performing your **role** within this Structure, Strategy or Composition, discuss **some** of the decisions you had to make during performance to ensure you carried out your role effectively.

6

(c) Describe the method(s) you used to gather information about your role when applying this Structure, Strategy or Composition.

4

(d) With reference to the information collected, describe a future development need and explain how this would improve your performance in the role you play.

4

(20)

Question 8

Choose an activity.

(a) Select a Structure, Strategy or Composition you have used. Explain the **benefits** that can be gained from applying this Structure, Strategy or Composition.

4

(b) Explain the **limitations** that have to be taken into account when applying this Structure, Strategy or Composition.

4

(c) Describe a performance situation that required you to **adapt or change** this Structure, Strategy or Composition. Explain why the adaptations/ changes were necessary.

6

(d) Describe how you evaluated the effectiveness of the adaptations/changes you made. Discuss the effects that these adaptations/changes had on your **overall** performance.

6

(20)

[END OF QUESTION PAPER]

[BLANK PAGE]

[BLANK PAGE]

X205/301

NATIONAL
QUALIFICATIONS
2007

FRIDAY, 25 MAY
9.00 AM – 11.30 AM

PHYSICAL
EDUCATION
HIGHER

Candidates should attempt **three** questions, each chosen from a different area.

SCOTTISH
QUALIFICATIONS
AUTHORITY

©

AREA 1: PERFORMANCE APPRECIATION

Marks

Question 1

Choose an activity.

(a) Describe the **nature** and **demands** of a quality performance within your selected activity.

6

(b) Mental factors can influence your performance. Explain how you were able to manage your emotions and mental state for a performance in your selected activity.

4

(c) When planning for performance improvement, discuss why it is important to use an **integrated training** (combination) approach to develop your whole performance. Give examples from your training programme to support your answer.

6

(d) Discuss why it is important to **monitor** and **review** your performance development.

4

(20)

Question 2

Choose an activity.

(a) Discuss the **positive** and **negative** influence of mental factors on performance.

4

(b) Technical, physical, personal and special qualities are important when performing. Select **three** of these qualities and explain their importance.

6

(c) Describe, in detail, the **strengths** and **weaknesses** in your whole performance in relation to **one** of the qualities you selected within part (b).

4

(d) Explain how you organised your training to **improve your weaknesses** whilst **maintaining your strengths**. Give examples from your training to support your answer.

6

(20)

AREA 2: PREPARATION OF THE BODY

Marks

Question 3

Choose an activity.

(*a*) Describe in detail the **range** of fitness requirements for effective performance. **6**

(*b*) Discuss why it is important to gather information about your **fitness**. **4**

(*c*) Training can take place:

- **within the activity (conditioning)**
- **outwith the activity**
- **through a combination of both.**

Select **one** of the above and briefly outline a training programme. Discuss why it was appropriate for you to train using the selected approach. **6**

(*d*) Having monitored your level of fitness during your training programme you will have made changes. Explain why these changes were necessary. Give examples to support your answer. **4**

(20)

Question 4

Choose an activity.

(*a*) Select an aspect of **skill related** fitness. Describe **one** method of gathering information on this aspect. Explain why this method was appropriate. **4**

(*b*) Explain the importance of **mental** fitness within an activity of your choice. **4**

(*c*) Discuss the importance of **setting goals** to improve your level of **physical** fitness. Give examples of the goals you set. **6**

(*d*) Discuss how you **planned** and **implemented** a training programme to achieve the goals set in part (*c*). **6**

(20)

[Turn over

AREA 3: SKILLS AND TECHNIQUES

Marks

Question 5

Choose an activity and a skill or technique.

(a) When learning and developing a skill, it is important to work through the three stages of learning. These are:

- **the preparation/cognitive stage**
- **the practice/associative stage**
- **the automatic/autonomous stage.**

Explain what you understand about **each** stage.   6

(b) Discuss why it is appropriate to use different methods of practice at **two different** stages of learning. Give examples from your programme of work to support your answer.   6

(c) Describe how you monitored your progress as you worked through your development programme.   4

(d) Having developed this skill/technique, discuss the **effect** that this has had on your **whole** performance.   4

(20)

Question 6

Choose an activity and a skill or technique.

(a) Describe the **features** of a skilled performance in this activity.   4

(b) When learning or developing a skill or technique, discuss the importance of **one** of the following:

(i) **Information Processing Model**
(ii) **Skill classification**.   4

(c) Describe, in detail, the **methods** you used to gather information on your level of performance. Explain why these methods were appropriate.   6

(d) From the information gathered, briefly describe a programme of work you used to develop this skill or technique. Explain why it is important to **review** your programme.   6

(20)

AREA 4: STRUCTURES, STRATEGIES AND COMPOSITION   *Marks*

Question 7

Choose an activity and a Structure, Strategy or Composition.

(a) Discuss why it is important to gather information about your performance when applying the Structure, Strategy or Composition. Give examples of the strengths and weaknesses you identified.   **6**

(b) Describe how you addressed the weaknesses highlighted in part (a). Explain the actions you took.   **4**

(c) When addressing your weaknesses you will have monitored your progress. Explain why this process is important.   **4**

(d) Structures, Strategies or Compositions are based on a number of key principles/fundamentals. For example:

- **speed in attack**
- **width/depth/mobility**
- **using repetition, variation and contrast**
- **the importance of creativity.**

Choose **two**, **either from your course or** from the list above and explain their importance when applying the Structure, Strategy or Composition.   **6**

                    (20)

Question 8

Choose an activity.

(a) Describe, in **detail**, a Structure, Strategy or Composition you have used.   **4**

(b) Discuss some of the **problems** that **either** you **or** your team/group experienced when applying this Structure, Strategy or Composition.   **6**

(c) With reference to the problems you experienced in part (b), discuss the **decisions** you took to develop and improve your performance.   **6**

(d) Explain how you evaluated any improvements that were made in your performance in the chosen Structure, Strategy or Composition.   **4**

                    (20)

[END OF QUESTION PAPER]

[BLANK PAGE]

[BLANK PAGE]

X205/301

NATIONAL
QUALIFICATIONS
2008

WEDNESDAY, 28 MAY
9.00 AM – 11.30 AM

PHYSICAL
EDUCATION
HIGHER

Candidates should attempt **three** questions, each chosen from a different area.

AREA 1: PERFORMANCE APPRECIATION

Marks

Question 1

Choose an activity.

(*a*) Describe in detail your personal performance in relation to **two** of the performance qualities listed below.

- **Technical**
- **Physical**
- **Personal**
- **Special**   6

(*b*) Select **one** of the qualities highlighted in Part (*a*). Describe in detail how you gathered information about this quality during your **overall** performance.   4

(*c*) Why is it important to use appropriate models of performance when developing your own performance?   4

(*d*) Discuss the importance of goal setting when planning your performance development. Give specific examples of the goals you set.   6

                                                      (20)

Question 2

Choose an activity.

(*a*) Explain what you understand about the **mental factors** which affect performance.   4

(*b*) Select a mental factor that had a negative effect on your performance. What method(s) did you use to overcome this difficulty? Why was the method(s) appropriate?   6

(*c*) Select a **weakness** within your whole performance. Discuss how you planned and managed a programme of improvement to develop your performance.   6

(*d*) Explain why it is important to review the effectiveness of your programme of improvement.   4

                                                      (20)

AREA 2: PREPARATION OF THE BODY

Marks

Question 3

Choose an activity.

(*a*) Describe the physical, skill related and mental fitness requirements for effective performance within your activity.

6

(*b*) From the fitness requirements described in Part (*a*), select **one** aspect. Explain how you gathered information about it **within** the activity.

4

(*c*) There are three phases of training:

- **preparation** (pre season)
- **competition** (during the season)
- **transition** (off season).

Discuss why your training might differ between **each** of the phases. Give examples to support your answer.

6

(*d*) Describe **one** method of training you used to develop your fitness. Explain why this method was appropriate.

4

(20)

Question 4

(*a*) Describe in detail a situation where your level of fitness:

(i) was a **strength** to your performance;

(ii) was a **weakness** to your performance.

(You may wish to answer this question through more than one activity.)

6

(*b*) With reference to either the strength or weakness identified in Part (*a*), describe in detail **one** method of training you used to develop your fitness.

4

(*c*) Discuss the **principles of training** you would consider when designing and completing a training programme.

6

(*d*) Explain why it is important to evaluate the effectiveness of your training programme.

4

(20)

[Turn over

AREA 3: SKILLS AND TECHNIQUES

Marks

Question 5

(a) Select **two** of the influential factors listed below.

- **Motivation**
- **Concentration**
- **Feedback**

Explain what you understand about each factor.　　　　6

Choose an activity and a skill or technique.

(b) Describe the programme of work that you followed to develop this skill or technique.　　　　4

(c) Discuss how the **principles of effective practice** were applied to the programme.　　　　6

(d) Explain how your whole performance was affected on completion of this programme of work.　　　　4

(20)

Question 6

Choose an activity and a skill or technique.

(a) Select **one** of the following approaches. Describe how you gathered information about your chosen skill or technique using this approach.

- **Mechanical analysis**
- **Movement analysis**
- **Consideration of quality**　　　　4

(b) Discuss the results of the information gathered in Part (a). Make specific reference to how your **whole** performance was affected.　　　　6

(c) Outline the programme of work that you followed to develop your performance in this skill or technique. Explain why this programme of work was appropriate.　　　　6

(d) Explain why it is important to monitor and review your programme of work.　　　　4

(20)

AREA 4: STRUCTURES, STRATEGIES AND COMPOSITION   *Marks*

Question 7

Choose an activity.

(a) Describe a Structure, Strategy or Composition that you have used. What were your strength(s) when applying this Structure, Strategy or Composition?   **6**

(b) Discuss how you planned your performance to make best use of your strength(s) when performing in this Structure, Strategy or Composition.   **4**

(c) Describe your weakness(es) when applying this Structure, Strategy or Composition. Discuss the effect that this had on your performance.   **6**

(d) Explain what you did to reduce the effect of the weakness(es) identified.   **4**

                                                                            (20)

Question 8

Choose an activity.

(a) Discuss the factors that you would take into consideration when selecting a Structure, Strategy or Composition.   **6**

(b) Describe in detail a Structure, Strategy or Composition that you have used.   **4**

(c) Briefly describe a situation where you had to **adapt or change** the Structure, Strategy or Composition in Part (b). Discuss why these changes or adaptations made your performance more effective.   **6**

(d) Having adapted or changed this Structure, Strategy or Composition, explain how you would evaluate its effectiveness.   **4**

                                                                            (20)

[END OF QUESTION PAPER]

[BLANK PAGE]

[BLANK PAGE]

[BLANK PAGE]

[BLANK PAGE]

[BLANK PAGE]

[BLANK PAGE]

[BLANK PAGE]

Pocket answer section for
SQA Higher Physical Education
2005–2008

© 2008 Scottish Qualifications Authority/Leckie & Leckie, All Rights Reserved
Published by Leckie & Leckie Ltd, 3rd Floor, 4 Queen Street, Edinburgh EH2 1JE
tel: 0131 220 6831, fax: 0131 225 9987, enquiries@leckieandleckie.co.uk, www.leckieandleckie.co.uk

Four model answers have been written for each exam in this book, one in each of the main Areas of the course (Performance Appreciation; Preparation of the Body; Skills and Technique; and Structures, Strategies and Composition). These model answers have been written by experienced teachers of PE and cover the most popular questions tackled in the exam. They should give you an indication of how you could write your own answers about your own activities.

The remaining 2005 exam questions have short marker guidelines. These are similar to the notes given to the examiners who mark the Higher PE exam. They focus on what should feature in a good answer. Remember though that these are only notes to guide you and should not be taken as an indication of the length of your answers in the final exam.

In the following, KU = Knowledge and Understanding

Physical Education
Higher SQP

SECTION 1: PERFORMANCE APPRECIATION

1. **Choose one activity.**

    (a) **Discuss both the challenges of this activity for you and the qualities you identified as your strengths and development needs.**

    Your answer should show knowledge of the relevant key concept and its application. This addresses the overall nature and demands of quality performance and technical, physical, personal and special qualities of performance.

    Your answer will depend upon the consideration of your selected activity and perhaps the specific role that you play within this activity. You must demonstrate knowledge and understanding about the specific challenges this presents for you and the qualities you possess. For example, I play football for my team; I have several technical, physical and mental challenges.... ....I cope well with the tough physical challenges that I get when players crowd in on me ......etc.... but feel that I need to do better when parrying the ball clear of danger....etc.
    You must also state clearly what you regard as your development needs.

    (b) **Choose one of the qualities discussed in part (a) which you identified as a development need. Describe the extent of the development need and exactly how it was identified.**

1. (b) **continued**

    You will need to give a full detailed description of the development need you identified. You must also demonstrate knowledge and understanding about how this weakness was identified-this will most likely be linked to one or more of the following methods which provides qualitative or quantitative detail:

    - Movement Analysis (Observation checklist, Match Analysis sheet)
    - Preparation/Action/Recovery: Mechanical Analysis of force, levers, propulsion etc
    - Consideration of Quality: reflecting on whether your skill or technique was controlled/fluent, or fast/slow?
    - Video – Comparison of your performance with that of a model performer. The video allowed playback, freeze frame.
    - Questionnaire: Questions should be relevant to and have responses such as 'done well', 'needs improvement' or mark your performance on a graded scale.

    Your development need may relate to personal/ team weakness which affects your own or team or both performances.
    For example, as a goalkeeper I am the last line of defence and responsible for "shutting out" goals... I must develop my technique of getting the ball clear and out of danger: too often I parry the ball back out into the penalty box where my opponents are ready to...etc. This puts tremendous pressure on my defenders... etc. As a result I am hesitant and slow to cover... My match analysis sheets show that too often I ...etc .. the video evidence backed this up showing that I would have been better to...etc.

    (c) **Awareness of performance weaknesses can be distracting during performance.**
    Discuss this statement with reference to the management of your performance and how model performers manage these situations.

    Your answer should show knowledge of the relevant key concept and its application. This addresses mental factors influencing performance, the use of appropriate models of performance and managing personal performance.

    Your answer should demonstrate critical thinking with an ability to show how your weaknesses affect you whilst you participate.
    By comparison the points made in your answer must highlight how model performers in the same situation would manage their performance.

Physical Education
Higher SQP (cont.)

1. (c) continued

When discussing how your performance weaknesses can distract you from performing to your best or prevents you performing your role effectively you may include some of the following points:
- reduces your confidence/motivation
- reduces your ability to select appropriate skills/decisions
- causes you to make unforced errors
- causes you to commit fouls
- affects the application of other skills
- makes you lose your temper/control/focus.

As you expand your answer you must highlight how model performers would cope in the same situation. Think about the points you have already used in the list above. The model performer will have the ability to be in full control of the performance with an ability to select, apply and adapt their skills as required to meet and do so without getting flustered. They will be in control of their emotions, be able to block out distractions, appear relaxed, confident and look effortless throughout.

(d) Discuss how you can plan and manage your performance improvement in the short and/or longer term?

You must demonstrate knowledge and understanding about the planning and managing process, i.e. that it is specific to your personal needs. Importantly, you must link this and demonstrate critical thinking as you explain how this will be done in the short and longer term. Your depth of answer will reflect some or all of the following:
- quality selected as a development need
- complexity of task
- stage of learning etc.
- identified short term target
- identified longer term target.

For example, your short term goal may be to be ready for your next game whilst your longer term target could be to maintain your 1st team position for the finals scheduled 6 months later.
Your answer may include consideration of managing your training in relation to some of the following considerations:
- practicing first in 'closed' situations, then progressing to more 'open' situations.
- training in or outwith the activity.
- principles of effective practice and/or principles of training.
- using game-like practices to reproduce pressures of actual games for example, include series of repetition and pressure drills to improve consistency.

2. Choose one activity.

(a) During your course you will have gathered data about different aspects of your whole performance in this activity. Discuss the significance of the information your data generated for two different aspects of your performance.

The data methods I used included the video, match analysis sheets and specific questionnaire sheet.
I wanted to find out how effective I was in my role as a wing defence in netball. Specifically, I wanted to know if I performed my defending and attacking duties consistently throughout the game. I decided to use the video as this was the best tool of analysis to avoid human error. The game is fast paced and I did not want to miss anything. The video allowed me to look at my game several times which let me check my match analysis and questionnaire sheets to see if they backed up what I was seeing.
The match analysis was divided into five minute slots for each of the four quarters. I asked my marker to indicate the number of passes I made, the number of passes I tipped or intercepted, the number of times I forced my partner to commit a foul or time violation, the number of unforced errors I made.
My questionnaire was designed specifically to evaluate my mental fitness. The specificity of the questions related to my success rate at controlling my temper; especially after making unforced errors or when the score was tight.
I was able to use these methods to define my strengths and weaknesses in my performance. The analysis of my data showed that I performed most of my defensive duties well. My percentages of interceptions, blocks and forced time violations were high; especially at the centre pass. I was not so consistent when performing my attacking duties, when our own GA and WA were being tightly marked. I should have been ready to get out and take this pass, instead I was slow to react to my centre requiring assistance and caused her to time violate. I was also mistiming my long feed into the circle and did not take enough notice of our opponents' GD; this meant I was throwing away potential shooting opportunities. I could see this first hand from the video action as I saw my poor ability to handle my emotions. This features as real weakness in my game and the results shown in my questionnaire reveal that on too many occasions I get caught up on poor umpire decisions, comments made by my opponents or indeed my dropped head and continual talking to myself when I make unforced errors.

2. (b) Discuss how you have used this information to develop a training programme to meet your identified needs. For each aspect of your performance give specific examples of what you did.

I used this information to help me design a training programme that would effectively suit my needs. I knew to consider specificity and so used a conditioning approach to my training which included a series of repetition – and game – related drills. This helped me to develop both my skill related fitness and mental aspects of my performance at the same time. I also found this more motivating and suited me best. As the nature of the game relies on a team effort it was essential that I practiced under similar game conditions. This helped me to produce a more consistent performance and helped me to adapt more quickly to the unexpected. I definitely needed to do something about my temper and it was suggested that I used 'self talk' to improve this. I was quite sceptical at this point! However the regime of deep breathing, focused thoughts and repeating in my head "Keep calm- don't say anything - no facial expressions - walk away" forced me to reflect on my game performance. I did this 3-5 times before my training and again at the end of each session.

In role related drills such as dodging/marking/throwing I made sure I worked under pressure; this improved my anticipation to cover space, reduce time and options for my opponent and heightened my awareness to move earlier to intercept. It also helped me to control my temper. For example, my coach told my WA to be quite aggressive and push me off the ball. Instead of reacting back or 'giving up' I took a deep breath mark and remained focussed; as a result I made greater effort to mark closer and press her.

The pressure drills of 'give and go' and 'box' practice were completed at various speeds. This again improved my anticipation and timing as I had to consider more than one cue at a time, for example, players were cutting into space sometimes 'open' sometimes 'marked', I was forced to consider options and make appropriate decisions. This was completed 3-5 times with a rest period in between.

I used repetition plays of set pieces such as centre passes, backline passes, side line throw-ins or penalty passes. This again forced me to practice my reaction time and anticipation in relation to the ball, the immediate situation and positioning of my team mates and the opposition. This helped sharpen my reaction speed, reinforced my passing accuracy and helped me to make better decisions. These plays were repeated 5 times first without opponents then with opponents to make it game like. I learned to respond to the 'unexpected' situations.

I made sure I varied the order of the drills, to make sure I did not get bored and took appropriate rests so that I did not get too tired.

2. (c) Describe how you managed your training over a period of time and explain any changes you made to your programme.

During my training period I knew to increase the intensity of my programme as I would have adapted to the previous one. I also did not want to become complacent as I feared I might slip back into old habits. I added different self talk statements so that I had a sequence of 3 different regimes I could use. This variation helped me to remain focused on controlling my temper. As well as doing this at the start and end of my training I would do it during rest periods as well; this helped me to reinforce new learned behaviour patterns. The more often I repeated these statements in my head the more calm and ready for action I seemed to become. The pressure drills were done more often and with more pressure added. For example, I would add in one more attacking player when doing my dodging/marking/throwing drill and did this 6-10 times – this helped me concentrate more.

I had learned that it was necessary to do more mass practice rather than distributed practice on occasions. I therefore changed the structure of the practice on occasions by ensuring a specific focus was made on one major area of weakness. For example, if our problem featured more on our centre pass play then I made sure we practised and concentrated solely on this for the biggest percentage of time. At other times I simply varied the drill order to avoid boredom or I would add increased pressure by adding in more players or simply increase the number of times the drill had to be completed.

The important factor about managing training over a period of time is the need to vary and adapt training to meet immediate requirements – I tried to do this.

(d) Describe how your training influenced your ability to meet the demands of performance in your chosen activity.

The biggest impact my training had was on my ability to control my temper. I noticed (and so did my team) a big improvement in my ability to manage my emotions. I was less likely to talk back at my own players or the umpire which meant I remained focused on what I was supposed to be doing. When I made a mistake I simply made myself more determined to get the ball back. I looked more positively at things and realised that the best way to attack was to be a more controlled player. Even when the game was tight I found myself encouraging players to get the ball back. This in turn led to improved statistics in my ability to make better decisions; I remained focused and contributed very positively to the game.

Very importantly this helped me to apply my other skills more effectively. Being more in control meant that I more effectively fulfilled my role related duties. My pressure and problem solving drills had made my anticipation sharper; as a result I moved to assist my team mates more consistently and was causing my opposite number to make more mistakes. I also took a split second more to time my passes and so made

Physical Education
Higher SQP (cont.)

2. (d) continued

fewer mistakes. My long feed passes directly into the shooting circle were more accurate as I was timing the pass well ahead of my GA and GS. I judged better the options available to me and made sure I used the safer short pass if the risky long ball was not on.

I consider myself a much more rounded player and know that I meet the demands of my role and the game much better than before.

SECTION 2: PREPARATION OF THE BODY

3. Choose an activity.

(a) Describe the methods you used to assess your fitness to meet the demands of performance in this activity. The activity chosen is badminton.

I first of all assessed my agility in badminton by doing the Illinois Agility Test which is an aspect of skill related fitness. Cones were placed on specific parts of the court and I had to follow a particular course as fast as possible. You start by lying face down on the floor and then on the command of 'Go' you are timed until you reach the finish. I did the test three times with a rest in between and the average time was taken for the three runs. I then compared my times to the national norms to see how agile I was.

Another method I used was the bleep test which is used to assess my physical fitness and in particular CRE which is important in badminton. This method was again a standard test where at the end I could compare my score against national norms to find out my level of CRE. This method involved running 20 metres in the games hall between two lines marked on the floor. I had to respond to a bleep noise from a tape. I had to run 20 metres and make the other line before the bleep sounded again. The bleeps became quicker as the time progressed and I had to keep running until I missed two consecutive bleeps. I then was given a score to compare to the national norms. The final method I used was a timed agility run which was set up on the badminton court. Four shuttles were placed on the singles court in the corners. On the signal 'Go' I had to place a shuttle from my starting point of central base and place it in the first corner and then return to central base to pick up another and then run to corner two and place it on the floor and then return to central base again. The same was done for corners three and four. After that I repeated the process in reverse until all four shuttles were returned to base. This was timed and gave me information on my reaction time and speed around the court as well as my agility.

(b) Use your knowledge and understanding to explain the principles that underpin progressive fitness training.

When you look at progressive fitness training there are certain principles which you must apply. Unless

3. (b) continued

the body is subjected to a certain level of stress its condition is unlikely to improve. Training must be progressive so that you gradually increase the stress you are placing on it. As you train you must adapt your fitness training so you can exercise at an increasingly higher level. The training first of all must be specific to you as well as specific for the activity you are taking part in. In order to make the training progressive I can apply various principles. These are: frequency, which is the number of sessions per week; the intensity, which means how hard I am working and the training loads per session; duration, which is the amount of time I am working in each session; and overload which is increasing the stress on my body. When I apply these to a progressive fitness training programme I can increase the frequency per week or the intensity I am working at or the amount of time I am training for. This then increases training and allows the body to adapt to this new stress and eventually it can cope with the new level of overload. If I want to keep improving my performance then I must again increase the level of overload that I place on it.

(c) Discuss one method of training you used and the advantages it offered for developing a specific type of fitness for performance in this activity.

The method of training I have selected is conditioning, which is training within the activity. The specific type of fitness I am going to develop is skill related fitness. By training within the activity I am able not only to improve those aspects of skill related fitness that are required to perform effectively in the game (for example agility, reaction time and co-ordination), but I am also able to practise and improve skills and movements around the court at the same time. Training on the court can be easily done and
this is advantageous as the work carried out can involve badminton – specific movements and also racquet drills that develop my skills as well as my fitness.

During the warm up I did some shadow drills involving running and returning to central base each time and the focus of this is relevant to the movements which I would do in a game situation. I also worked without a shuttle which allowed me to concentrate on the steps which I would use during a game. I then carried out some feeder then repetition practices which again allowed me to work on skills as well as skill related fitness and finally I did some pressure practices. Training in this way is important in creating the real fitness demands of a competitive match and is much more enjoyable to take part in. Another advantage of this type of training is that it keeps you motivated because you are training on the badminton court and are able to practise and play by doing actual badminton related skills and games. Increased levels of motivation lead to a desire to improve and a will to do well. You also do not need any specialist equipment so it is easy to organise and carry out.

3. continued

(d) Discuss how you applied the principles of training identified in Part (b) in planning and carrying out the training method you used. Support your discussion with specific examples from your training programme.

The first principle I applied when planning and carrying out my fitness programme was specificity as I made sure after having gathered information on my level of fitness that my programme was based on badminton and on the type of fitness that I wanted to improve, which was skill related fitness. I planned a training programme by training through the activity and would carry out a series of drills which would not only improve my skill related fitness but my skills in the game as well.

I planned an initial eight week training programme based on my previous results from the methods used to gather information on my fitness. I would carry out my training during my PE periods for two × 1 hour periods per week. I monitored my training from session to session and after about three to four weeks I began to see some improvements. I then started to increase my work load so that I would continue to improve.

During my training I used court – based exercise drills designed to improve my agility. I also did shadow drills and skill based pressure drills which developed my fitness. I did all my training drills in sets. For example I worked to and from my central base to return overhead clears fed to the back corners of the court. I did one set of 8 to each corner and did two sets of this drill with a 45 second rest between each set carried out. As my fitness improved, in order to progress I increased the number of sets to three that I did in my training in weeks four and five and later in the programme also reduced the recovery time between sets to 35 seconds. This ensured progression within the programme and put my body under more stress therefore improving all aspects of my work. I also was able to train for three times per week so I was also increasing the frequency of my training. By using these principles my programme was progressive. Training in this way within the activity was enjoyable and a relevant way of improving my skill related fitness together with developing my skills.

4. Choose an activity.

(a) Use your knowledge and understanding to discuss why one aspect of each of the following types of fitness is needed for successful performance in the chosen activity.
- **physical fitness**
- **skill related fitness**
- **mental fitness**

Your answer should show knowledge of the relevant key concept and its application. This addresses physical, skill related and mental types of fitness. The answer must have one aspect of fitness from each type.

4. (a) continued

Physical fitness could be
- CRE
- Strength
- Local muscular endurance
- Flexibility
- Speed
- Power.

An example would be in swimming over 400 metres front crawl, local muscular endurance is needed. As you swim over 16 lengths there is continuous demand for your arm and leg muscles to be working. Your body needs to cope with this continuous action and the higher level of muscular endurance you have the more efficient the stroke will be before fatigue sets in.

Skill related fitness. An example should be taken from:
- Agility
- Reaction time
- Balance
- Timing
- Co-ordination
- Movement anticipation.

Mental fitness. An example should be taken from:
- Level of arousal
- Rehearsal
- Managing emotions.

(b) Choose one of the aspects of fitness you identified in Part (a). Discuss your knowledge of fitness assessment methods in relation to this aspect of fitness and the information different methods can provide.

Your answer should show knowledge of the relevant key concept and its application. This addresses fitness assessment in relation to personal performance and the demands of activities.

You must select one of the aspects of fitness from part (a) and discuss the fitness assessment methods you could use. For example: aspect selected: muscular endurance

I had a partner gather information on my stroke count when swimming 16 lengths to see how many strokes I took for each two lengths to see if my stroke deteriorated towards the end.

Depending on aspect selected various methods could be used. These could include:
- Standard fitness tests
- Video
- Observation schedule
- Questionnaire
- Criteria check list.

Methods could provide information on:
- Your level of fitness
- Level of ability
- Strengths and weaknesses
- Focus for future planning
- Starting point for your training programme.

Physical Education
Higher SQP (cont.)

4. (c) continued

Describe, in detail, the content of a training programme where you focused on the aspect of fitness identified in Part (b) to develop your performance.

Your answer should show detail about a training programme based on the aspect of fitness selected in part (b).

You should describe the method of training you are using and give details of the content which should take into account the principles of training.

The programme could show detail of:
- Length of time your are working
- How long each session should last
- Types or exercises being done
- Progression
- Overload
- Intensity of work
- Specificity.

(d) Choose one of the other aspects of fitness you identified in Part (a). For this aspect discuss your future training needs to further develop your performance.

Your answer should show evidence of another aspect of fitness identified from part (a) and identify future needs.

For example, in swimming I have selected mental fitness and the aspect of rehearsal. My training needs would be to try and become more relaxed during races and not let the pressures get to me when performing. This I could achieve by learning how to relax before races; by going through in my mind how I am going to swim the race and what tactics I am going to use and trying to focus my mind on the task ahead.

SECTION 3: SKILLS AND TECHNIQUE

5. Choose an activity.

(a) Describe some of the features of performance that can be identified at each of the stages of skill learning. Give specific examples from the chosen activity.

Your answer should show knowledge of the relevant key concept and its application. This addresses the development of skill and the refinement of technique.

The depth of your answer must offer a sound description with full details and exhibit detailed KU about relevant features related to each of the three stages of learning. Your responses should include specific and personal examples related to an activity. For example, at the cognitive stage (planning stage) performance is just recognisable and often looks clumsy/awkward, movements look rushed and are not controlled or fluent and there is total lack of consistency. There is little evidence of a wide repertoire of skills with a very poor level of decision making when applying skills in whole performance.

5. (a) continued

At the associative stage (preparation stage) performance looks reasonably comfortable, movements are more recognisable and there is some degree of control and fluency beginning to show. There is greater consistency with evidence of a repertoire of skills developing, some good decision making is apparent when applying skills in whole performance.

At the automatic stage (autonomous stage) performance looks skilled, controlled and fluent. There is a feeling of having plenty of time when applying skills with a high degree of consistency. A full range of skills to meet performance demands is apparent with a high level of decision making used throughout performance.

(b) Select a skill or technique from your activity. Give a detailed analysis of the features of your performance that clearly mark out your current stage of learning.

Your answer must demonstrate critical thinking and show knowledge and understanding about your current level of performance. The examples you give will reflect the activity you have selected.

For example, in swimming, a technique I am trying to learn is my tumble turn... I am at the cognitive stage and feel I will never be able to perform it well..., I find it really hard to control and I am scared I will bump my head on the wall when... I fail to tuck right round and end up facing the wrong way... if I do get round I am often too far away from the wall to push off... My timing needs to be better when I approach the wall and I...

For example, in hockey a technique I am trying to perfect is my flick shot... I am at the associative stage and feel I can perform it quite well..., I am accurate using the flick shot when performing in isolation ... I have a fair shooting success rate but in a full game I lack... I can shoot from different angles but I am not so successful from my left... I hurry the shot and do not often play it at the right time...

For example, in football a technique I am extremely confident in using is my dribbling... I am at the automatic stage and feel I can perform it very well..., I am accurate and can take on more than one player...when ... I can approach my opponents from different angles and easily disguise my intent... I am very successful and always in control... this creates opportunities for me as I have more space and time on the ball this also ... I am confident at all times and use this skill at the right time...

(c) When developing this skill or technique, discuss how you used your knowledge of skill learning to design an appropriate programme of work. Give specific details of the programme you used.

Your answer should show knowledge of the relevant key concept and its application. This addresses the development of skill and the refinement of technique.

For example, when trying to perfect my flick shot I thought about the level I was at and what I was going to achieve... I considered my short and long term

5. (c) continued

goals… I knew not to use too many shadow practices as these are better suited to the cognitive stage … I knew at the associative stage I would need to use a lot of repetition drills to make sure I got more familiar and consistent at it… I knew that I would get bored if my practices were too easy therefore I knew to progress the degree of difficulty by… I also introduced more game like practices by including a series of combination and problem solving drills. This would help me… at the associative stage. I still need plenty of feedback as I am not good enough to pinpoint where in my sub routines I may be going wrong… I need to set targets such as I had to score at least 6 out of 10 attempts before…

(d) Describe how you evaluated the effectiveness of the programme you used.

Your answer must demonstrate related KU and critical thinking in relation to how you used different methods to evaluate the effectiveness of your programme.

For example, on completion of my practice programme I evaluated how effective it was by making comparisons about my game performance and percentage shooting rate… I compared these current match statistics to my initial performance… I also used the video and found this to be the most appropriate in terms of motivation and simplicity to use… The video captured the action as it happened, thus avoiding human error… After reviewing the video I was able to evaluate the quality and control of my flick shot and make qualitative judgements … I was able to back this up from the supportive data contained in my match analysis sheets by examining the quantitative evidence. … I also relied on my own opinion about the improvements I made in terms of accurate shots against number of attempts made and whether or not I had reached my personal short and long term goals… if I had made improvements then I judged that the programme I had set up was pitched at the correct level for me.

6. (a) Explain, in detail, what you understand about information processing and its relevance to learning and developing skill or refining technique.

Briefly, information processing involves reaction to a stimulus whereby the brain sends a message to the muscles to ensure action takes place. The brain makes sense of the action taken and the whole process starts again. This diagram shows how it works.

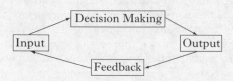

I appreciate that when I am learning skills or refining my technique that this process happens extremely quickly with all 4 parts linked together. Firstly, at the input stage I receive information (known as stimulus or cue); this could be an instruction from my coach or

6. (a) continued

movement by my team-mate/opponent. Secondly, based on this information I must make sense of it i.e. assimilate it and make a decision about what action I am going to make. For example, when learning a skill: (serve) I might want to repeat the action several times to make sure I get the whole action correct. For example, the use of feeder drills would help. However in a game situation I do not have a lot of time to think about what I am going to do and I have to act very quickly. I might think about where on the court I will place my serve; slice, flat or topspin? Thirdly, is the output i.e. how I have responded to the decision made – having angled my serve cross court – did I get ready to move in to volley? The last part reflects how effective my decision was, for example, did I win the point i.e. an ace or was it returned? – based on this outcome the whole process starts again instantaneously.

I have learned that this is a continuous process and the more experienced you are the better you are at it. It takes lots of practice to develop and good performers can do it automatically. Information processing relies on a lot of other factors such as previous learned experiences, timing, reaction time and anticipation. Previous experience counts for a lot because the more experiences you have, the better your timing becomes and you learn to react and anticipate what is going to happen. This gives you more available options; which means better decision making.

I have also learned that when learning a new skill, or refining a complex skill, I have to rely on information from different senses: touch, vision, verbal etc. For example, in this situation I need to rely a lot on verbal and visual instruction as this helps me to make sense of what I am being asked to do. I am able to get the feel for the technique and get good feedback to help me to progress or correct any errors. When the skill is familiar to me I am able to rely on my own kinaesthetic feedback and effectively refine the sub routines of the skill or apply the skill in a game situation. I have also learned that to improve my skill level I have to simultaneously develop my ability to process information. This relies on my ability to take in important information and ignore irrelevant information. The best way to do this is to practise with model performers and to use conditioned or pressure drills.

(b) Select a complex skill or technique from an activity of your choice. When developing or refining or applying this skill or technique, discuss the range of information you had to process to ensure your performance improved.

In tennis, I have worked hard to develop my service, basically because this can be your most valuable weapon. Many of today's great players rely on a well placed first serve (and can often win the rally with an ace) and if unsuccessful they can confidently place their second service. I serve reasonably consistently but when required to place it I can be inconsistent. Executing an ace is extremely difficult but I endeavour to do this using as much power behind the ball as I can as this puts me at a strategic advantage

Physical Education
Higher SQP (cont.)

6. (b) continued

and puts my opponent under immediate pressure. Selecting the correct type of serve to deliver depends on experience i.e. topspin, slice or flat and this is a high quality skill in itself. If I am forced to use my second serve this is not as reliable as I have to worry about placement rather than speed – this causes the ball to 'play short' and I present my opponent with an easy opportunity to attack. Placing my serve requires me to use different techniques such as topspin, flat or sliced. The selection of which type I will use depends on various things; first and foremost is this first or second serve? Where is my opponent positioned? Are they a strong backhand player? What is the weather like, sunny or windy? What stage in the game I am at, the balls used may be old or I may have just had a ball change. Once I know my game scenario, in other words I have processed the information available to me, I can then select which service to use. I favour the flat serve as this is more directed at my opponent's body and has a low, powerful trajectory. I know from previous experience what kind of return to expect from my opponent and I am ready to respond to their shot selection. Each time I serve I watch how my opponent copes with it and if need be I vary the technique to ensure I apply pressure and ensure that I remain effective and gain the upper hand.

(c) Describe, in detail, the methods of practice which you used to improve your ability in the chosen skill or technique with a view to improving your whole performance.

To refine my technique I used a series of progressive practices. Firstly, this involved the use of repetition drills where I aimed at targets placed at the base of the serve box; left/centre/ right. This was in a 'closed' situation as I did not need to worry about the returned shot. This gave me a visual picture of the correct action and placement of my serve. I learned at this stage to reinforce my ball toss action, body positioning and follow through action. I also learned to adapt all of the aforementioned factors according to the type of serve selected. Depending on which target I was aiming at would reinforce my ability to place and vary the tempo and depth of my serve – my ball toss is important here. Feedback during these repetitive drills came mainly from myself – the 'feel' of the action. If I missed the deep corner targets then I simply aimed to get the ball any where in the serve box for my second serve; this took pressure off me. I repeated this several times making sure I aimed at each target 10 times. I monitored my success rate and rested before I repeated the drill from the left-hand side of the court. This was necessary to ensure I was effective on both sides.

I progressed using pressure drills, firstly I used the ball feed machine. Here I could adjust the speed and direction of the return which helped to develop my follow up attacking play. I used this for a short time only as I got bored too easily by this. I progressed to using partner pressure drills as I found this much

6. (c) continued

more challenging. Playing a person rather than a machine made the pressures more like the real thing. Basically I found myself much more motivated to do well as I liked watching the response made by my partner as they worked to return my serve. Watching their positioning was much more beneficial to my development than playing the machine as I had to learn to make better decisions and selections quicker in direct response to what my partner opted to do. The game- like nature developed my ability to make better decisions. The unpredictable responses made by my partner made me more alert and ready to respond with my follow up action, which could be to move in to volley or stay back and engage in a baseline rally. During these drills I was also able to develop other types of my fitness at the same time such as my agility, timing and reaction time. I was also able to develop my mental fitness which is a very important aspect of the serve. I learned to control my emotions, fully concentrate on the task on hand and block out any unnecessary distractions. This also helped me not to panic when I 'double served'. The 'open nature' of this practice helped me to internalise how the serve should feel when played under pressure: this prepared me more for the game and helped me to instinctively attack right from the start. I was now much more confident of getting that very necessary first serve in.

(d) Describe in detail, how you monitored your progress during practice. Explain what you did to ensure your progress was continuous.

I used several methods to monitor my progress during practice. Firstly I used my initial target drill percentages to allow me to make comparisons. During my training I could see which of the techniques – topspin, slice or flat I had more success with. I could also tell whether I was better on the right or left hand side of the court and also relied on my kinaesthetic feedback as I developed a better sense of 'knowing' when I had hit a good serve. I could feel and see improvements, for example, when I felt I had placed a wide and deep topspin serve I knew to quickly follow in and finish the rally with a strong punch volley – this was happening more frequently.

I also filmed my performance during practice and match sessions to let me see first hand how I looked and where on the court I favoured placement. I could also rewind this and get feedback on errors featuring as problems on any of the subroutines of my action. Part of my monitoring process was to talk over with my coach what I saw when we replayed the tape. I found this motivating as my coach encouraged me to vary the serve and take in more of the game cues such as positioning of my opponent on court and so learn to adjust and vary my serve selection more effectively.

The most obvious indicator was my match statistics. By comparing my previous game stats I was able to examine first serves won, double fault errors and percentage serve placements etc.

I used all of these methods to help me to plan appropriate practice and ensure I progressed. I

6. (d) continued

highlighted areas of weakness and could use regulated court practice to ensure I got more ace serves in and so win games in three sets rather than being pushed into a punishing five setter.

SECTION 4: STRUCTURES, STRATEGIES AND COMPOSITION

7. (a) Choose an activity and a structure, strategy or composition you have used. Describe how you planned your practice of this structure, strategy or composition to ensure you were prepared to apply and adapt it as performance circumstances required.

The activity I have selected is basketball and the strategy I used was the fast break. When you practise you try to put into operation the actual SSC that you are going to use in a game so it is important to relate practices and drills which will help to make all the team familiar with their roles in the strategy. Also it is important to come up with a change or changes within the strategy because in a game as a team you are faced with opposition who may be able to prevent successful carrying out of this strategy or you may find part of it is breaking down and you still want to use the same strategy but you need to be able to adapt it depending on the circumstances you are faced with. When we planned our practice we needed to apply the strategy as a team and make sure that every person knew their role within it. As a group, our teacher went over the fast break on the whiteboard so we were clear what the strategy involved was. We then identified positions for people in the class based on their particular strengths and weaknesses previously identified. We then created a training programme with game like situations for practices. First of all we walked through the fast break several times unopposed so that every person became familiar with their role and function. We then performed it faster until we were doing it at game pace. We then moved on to a 3v1 drill where we were faced with one active defender who started off court at the top of their key and could only become active once the outlet pass had been made. From there we then played 3v2 where the first defender started at the top of their key and, once as a three we had passed the ball to one of our forwards (a second defender, who was positioned at the half way line), could then become active. This practice encouraged us to use the extra players we had in the overload we had created before the other defender came into play. We then progressed to a 3v2 with a delayed defender similar to the previous drill. These drills made us face different game like situations and also improved our decision making at the same time. Finally we played 3v3 where we had to fast break as much as possible. All these drills and practices allowed us as a team to build up the fast break, become familiar with our roles and be able to apply this as a team. However, as a team we know when we are playing that the opposition will become familiar with the simple fast break (consisting of outlet pass, dribble down middle and then pass to a forward to score a lay up) so as a team we also have to practise how we could adapt the fast break to give us options as a team

7. (a) continued

and make the opposition react accordingly. Therefore as a group we practised how we could adapt the fast break. This involved a simple change at the final part of the break so we could make alternative passes or reverse the ball for another player to shoot. Again we practised this as a team using the drills we had used before but using the adaptations we had come up with. This would ensure in a game if certain situations occurred as a team we could still carry out our strategy and could adapt where necessary.

(b) When using this structure, strategy or composition describe how your strength(s) and weakness(es) influenced your practice and performance.

When using any strategy it is important that you gather information on your performance within a game so you are able to find out your strengths and weaknesses. This will then give you a starting point for your training to be based on. You want to build on your strengths as a team and use them to the best of your ability and improve any weaknesses which you might have. This will have a big influence on your training. When we played against two other schools in a tournament we found out by taking data on the effectiveness of the strategy that our strengths were that we were good at starting the break off and were good at dribbling the ball down the middle. Our weaknesses were we were poor at timing the pass to the forward and often the opposition intercepted the ball and counter – attacked us. Also we were poor at the final part or the break which was the lay up from one of the forwards. We would miss the lay up or the forward was tightly marked and then could not drive past the defender to the basket. This meant we then had to set the ball up and try to score via another play.

Therefore when we came to practise we made sure that we continued to practise all the parts of the fast break not just the parts which we were struggling with. We based our training programme on drills which were game like as it is important to try and practice as close to the actual game as possible. Also it was important to try and practise the adaptations which we could use when the forward was unable to do the lay up so that we could use this when necessary.

(c) Discuss how you adapted your performance in this structure, strategy or composition to reduce the effect of your weakness(es). Explain, in detail, the adaptations you made to minimise identified weakness(es).

We adapted the performance in the fast break based on the weaknesses which we had identified from our data gathered whilst playing. Our weaknesses were identified as the final pass to the forward being poor and the forward being trapped with the ball at the side because the opposition became familiar with our fast break. As a team we went back and practised the weaknesses identified but also practised working on adapting the strategy. The adaptations we made were to try and still use the basic fast break but adapt it so we could use another play if it broke down.

Physical Education
Higher SQP (cont.)

7. (c) continued

We decided that when the person dribbling the ball down the middle received the ball he could pass the ball earlier to one of the forwards out wide who would then draw the defender towards him and then play a cross court pass when he reached the top of the opposition's key to our other forward who would then drive to the basket. By passing earlier we would surprise the opposition and pull the defenders to the ball and hopefully create space for the other forward. The other adaptation we made was to apply the normal fast break until the dribbler reached the top of the key and passed the ball to one of the forwards. If this forward was marked he would fake a shot and reverse pass the ball back to the dribbler who had stepped closer to the basket. This person should now be able to shoot close to the basket or drive to the basket or pass to the opposite forward at the side. This then gave us various options from the original fast break. This would hopefully catch the opposition off guard and allow us to score a basket and overcome the problem we faced of the forward being trapped at the side with few options available. Again we practised this in training so we became familiar with the changes. Because we could now adapt the fast break depending on the circumstances we faced the opposition found it much harder to defend as we now had different options available.

(d) As a result of the adaptations you made, describe how you evaluated the effectiveness of the performance. Identify one future development need within this structure, strategy or composition.

We evaluated the effectiveness of our performance by using a video to record our matches. From this we could see whether our fast break was working effectively and if and when we used the adaptations that they were working as well. Using a video gave us the opportunity to look back on and freeze the play and point out good or bad points, it also gave us the chance to study the opposition to see how they reacted to our strategy. This also gave us the opportunity to compare our performance to that of previous games which, if we had improved, was really good for team morale as we could see all our hard work in practice had paid off. If some parts still needed improvement it gave us the chance to see it on film. We also made up an observation schedule where all the parts of the fast break were identified. One of our class who was not playing marked a tick or a cross against the criteria every time we used the fast break. From this information we could then compare to previous results to see if we had improved and whether or not the adaptations had worked and also how often we actually used this. This provided hard evidence which was valid and reliable. One future need which we identified was that we had to still improve our lay up shooting at the end of the break and also the shooting of the person who received the reverse pass in our adaptation in the fast break. Often we would appear to have an unopposed shot but we continued to miss more often than not.

8. (a) Describe, in detail, a structure, strategy or composition that you would usually select as your first choice. Explain why you would select this structure, strategy or composition in preference to any other.

Your answer should show knowledge of the relevant key concept and its application when analysing and developing performance. This addresses structures, strategies and compositional elements that are fundamental to activities.

Your answer must include a detailed description of a structure, strategy or composition which you have used. It should have detail of the aim. For example in football we use the 3-5-2 formation. This structure has 3 defenders playing at the back with one centre back that is responsible for the middle of the defence. The other two defenders cover the right and left side of the defence but are helped out by the two wingbacks that are the outside players in the midfield …etc.

You must explain why you would use this structure. For example:

- Type of players we have in term of strengths and weaknesses
- Ability of certain players
- Attacking qualities that are provided
- Defensive qualities provided
- Flexibility it allows
- Principles of play covered in terms of width, depth and mobility
- Type of system played by opponents.

(b) Discuss the importance of developing alternative structures, strategies or compositions when practising to meet less predictable performance demands.

Your answer should show knowledge of the relevant key concept and its application when analysing and developing performance. This addresses structures, strategies and compositional elements that are fundamental to activities.

Your answer should mention the type of alternative SSC you would develop.

Your answer may also describe the situation you are faced with.

For example 4-4-2 in football. You must also say why it is important to develop alternatives.

For example when playing football you will come up against situations which just happen. The opposition might play a man to man marking of particular players which you have not come up against before so it is important that you are able to combat that by being able to change or adapt the original SSC. It is important therefore you have practised this in training. Having done this you can then hopefully overcome the problem you are faced with.

Other answers could include:

Circumstances you are faced with

Stage of the game

Result at the time

Substitution of players.

8. continued

(c) **During the application of a structure, strategy or composition focusing your attention on relevant information can ensure that effective decisions are made.**
With reference to the role you played or a performance you planned give examples of two pieces of information you would look for to help inform your decision making.

Your answer should include a description of the role you played or the performance you planned.
For example my role in the 3-5-2 was the right wide midfield player whose role was to support the forwards when attacking and track back to help the defence when the opposition were attacking.
Types of information to inform your decision making may include reference to
  • Number of successful runs up the wing
  • Most effective pass I could use
  • How many times I lost my player when defending
  • Success of the SSC
  • My ability to link with my team mates and play as a coherent unit
  • Position of team mates when I have the ball.

(d) **Discuss how you would organise your future training to ensure you had opportunities to practice decision-making when applying structures, strategies or compositions.**

Your answer should make reference to suggestions about your programme of work.
When organising future training, reference should be made to the type of practices or drills you may use that allows decision making to take place.
For example you may play small sided games to apply pressure to players.
You may practice particular set plays you use within the SSC.
You may practice against a particular set play you are faced with in a game.
You may play conditioned games with certain restrictions.

Physical Education Higher 2005

AREA 1: PERFORMANCE APPRECIATION

1. **Choose an activity.**

(a) **Discuss the qualities that you consider to be strengths in your performance.**

In Basketball I feel I have a wide range of qualities that enable me to perform my role effectively. As a power forward I have good physical qualities such as cardio respiratory endurance which helps me to work hard throughout the duration of the game. I have very good explosive power and I win many rebounds, which is a real advantage if I miss my shot. When defending I mark very tightly and force my opponents into making mistakes. Being agile and having good timing and anticipation helps me cut and penetrate into the key. I have good mental qualities such as controlling anxiety which helps me keep calm and so I make good decisions when under pressure. This also stops me from making careless passes or fouling. I feel I have special qualities which make me a difficult player to contend with. I can easily 'fake & go' and so wrong foot my opponent; I enjoy having my opponent constantly under pressure with the feeling that I am very much in control. I feel I have excellent technical qualities and am very consistent when passing, dribbling and shooting. My game statistics are high and reasonably consistent and I contribute much to the success of my team. I am a competitive player and do not like to get beaten, therefore I make sure I communicate with my teammates and ensure that they work hard even if we are trailing by a few baskets. I feel I inspire them as I rarely give up.

(b) **Describe how you planned to improve two different areas of your performance in this activity over a specified period of time.**

In the short term, I planned to keep my general fitness and technical abilities sharp by attending my normal weekly training sessions. I trained 3 times a week in preparation for our league matches. In these sessions, I used a variety of training methods but mainly relied on a conditioning approach. Specific drills were used in the form of a 6 station circuit aimed at improving my cardio respiratory and speed endurance whilst improving my role related duties of passing, dribbling and shooting etc. I moved around each station working at 75% of my work rate intensity and ensured I was in my training zone. I took 1 minute rest periods after each rep and recorded the number of passes, dribbles and shots made so that I knew my own targets. At the end of each session I got feedback on my progress and always finished with 1v1 or 2v1 basket drives to help improve my game skills, this kept me motivated as I enjoyed the challenge.
In the longer term, I planned for greater improvements and ensured my fitness, skill and technical abilities were well developed for the District championships. The championships were a four day event and involved us playing at least four games a day. Sometimes we were drawn back to back and had

Physical Education
Higher 2005 (cont.)

1. (b) continued

to play another team with only a 'change of court' rest period. This made tremendous demands on us physically and mentally and our preparation had to be pretty extensive. We had to be loyal and dedicated to team practice and work hard on our individual fitness and skills as well as work co-operatively as a team on repetitive practice drills of our preferred strategies. As well as my other teammates I had a specific individual training programme that I had to follow as well as attending team practice. At this time I trained outwith the activity and I took responsibility for this myself. For example, I went out running (at least 20 mins) and completed a fartlek circuit twice a week; this improved my cardio respiratory and speed endurance. This was over and above team training. At training I completed an individual skill and shooting circuit and then with the rest of the squad practiced different strategies that we felt we would use in our matches. I needed to be patient as our coach always swapped us in and out to make sure the best five were matched to the strategy adopted. Fortunately, my skills and fitness are excellent and I am regarded as one of the key players therefore I rarely got any rest, I was always involved. I did not mind this hard work as it helped me to cope with game pressures as I was always being pushed to the limit. The training duration was over a 3 month period. These championships were very important to us as qualification meant an invite to the Regional finals. There was no better incentive in my planning than wanting to be part of this big arena; all the hard work over this long period I felt would definitely be worth it.

(c) Describe how you monitored your progress during training. Explain the impact the training had on your performance.

During my training I monitored my progress in various ways. In the short term I simply recorded my success rate at my skills on completion of each station. This gave me a personal record which I compared to previous targets. This was motivating as I was determined always to do better, especially in my shooting and rebounding drills. This training improved my success rate percentages during my practice games. I felt much more comfortable when participating in tight matches and felt I was coasting at times. My speed around the court improved and I found it easier to assist play and cut into the key and score baskets.

In the longer term I still used targets as an accurate way of affirming improvements. As a result of overloading my running and fartlek programme I felt I could give an extra burst of speed when closing down opponents and when switching from offence to defence duties. I knew that I was performing my role much more consistently. As a result of scrutinising video footage (an excellent source for valid feedback) I could see firsthand that I was causing my opponents real problems in and around the key: my work rate caused my opposite number to make

1. (c) continued

contact fouls which was very pleasing. I also used feedback from coach and team-mates who commented on my play when we compared game statistics. I maintained a greater passing distribution I feel because I had the fitness to cope with greater game involvement. I made more steals and contributed more in all areas of the court. Due to the repetitive nature of our fastbreak drills, we had improved our speed and reaction time at setting this up and so completed it faster; we effectively gave our opponents no time and won by a greater margin. I feel this proves that my training had a very positive impact on my performance.

(d) Discuss how you used models of performance to evaluate the development of your performance.

I often used model performers when evaluating my performance. In my squad there were two players who were much better than me and I aspired to be as good as them. During training I would watch their shooting technique and copy them to improve my own. I always worked with them so that I could compare my drill statistics against theirs. I loved this level of direct competition and used this as a form of target setting; this kept me motivated and determined to do better. When we were completing our running and fartlek training I tried my best to keep up with them. I found this difficult at first but it gradually got easier as I became fitter. However, I still felt that in the speed department I had a bit of work to do. My team-mates gave me encouragement and valuable feedback and commented that I seemed to be getting better. This was a great benefit to me. We would often challenge each other to a race at the end of sessions and although I did not win, at least I was not last; plus my times were getting faster.

After games we watched video footage which helped me to look at my overall effectiveness compared to theirs; I got different ideas on how to better my 'fake and go' moves and so it gave me more options and I learned to be more creative. Further observation highlighted that my shooting had greatly improved. I was now much more balanced and released the ball much earlier so had increased my game averages. Evaluating my performance both qualitatively and quantifiably to the model performers helped me accurately judge improvements and identify areas of my performance still requiring attention.

2. Choose an activity.

(a) Describe how you obtained data about two different areas of your whole performance. What information about specific development needs did your data provide?

Your answer should demonstrate Knowledge and Understanding in relation to one or more related methods. For example, you may have used different methods of analysis which are relevant to general and focused data. The methods selected may include qualitative or quantitative detail in relation to a selected skill or technique/fitness; general or specific etc. The information should include a brief

2. (a) continued

description and offer relevant details of associated criteria. Examples may include:

- Movement Analysis: (Observation checklist, Match Analysis sheet)
- Preparation/Action/Recovery: Mechanical Analysis of force, levers, propulsion etc
- Consideration of Quality: reflecting on whether your skill or technique was controlled/fluent, or fast/slow
- Video: Comparison of your performance with that of a model performer. The video allowed playback, freeze frame.
- Questionnaire: Questions should be relevant to and have responses such as 'done well', 'needs improvement' or mark your performance on a graded scale.

Your answer must include evaluative comments about what the data highlighted means in relation to the strengths and weaknesses of your performances. For example, a review of the video showed that I had excellent technique and … Results from my questionnaire suggested that I am competent in the execution of my simple skills but less consistent when I perform complex skills like… etc.

(b) Outline the training programme you planned to meet your development needs.

Your answer should show knowledge of the key concept and its application. This addresses planning and managing personal performance improvement.

For example, the training would be game-like (to reproduce pressures of actual games) and would include a series of repetition and pressure drills because these are specific to reproducing consistency/creativity in whole performance situations. You may also make reference to completing your training in or outwith the activity via a conditioning approach or via circuit, weight or fartlek training. Your answer should also include considerations of principles of effective practice and/or principles of training.

You must give specific details from the actual programme used.

(c) Justify the relevance of the training you planned. Explain any adaptations you made over the time.

Your answer must demonstrate critical thinking and show knowledge and understanding about the specificity of the training method(s) selected. For example, I selected to train both in and outwith the activity because… or I selected to use a conditioning approach because…

You must include examples of the adaptations you made showing progression and explain in detail why you made the adaptations. For example: as I got faster at this circuit I made my running distance longer and took a smaller rest period… or Now that I could get 15/15 baskets I increased the number to 20 from three different areas around the basket before I moved on… This made me focus more therefore I… etc.

Your answer may also include detail in relation to improved performance.

2. (d) Discuss the value of setting goals when planning training to develop your performance.

Your answer should show knowledge of the relevant key concept and application. This addresses planning and managing personal performance improvement. For example, goals set will help you to

- set short/long term training targets
- reach personal achievement
- reflect success/monitor improvements
- judge training benefits
- remain motivated/determined/committed
- make future goals

As you develop your answer you must give specific examples of using some of the above. For example, as I had reached my personal target of getting 8/12 putts in I felt a great sense of achievement and knew I was improving… etc.

AREA 2: PREPARATION OF THE BODY

3. Choose an activity. The activity chosen is basketball.

(a) Physical, skill-related and mental fitness are all required for successful performance. With reference to your chosen activity, explain why one aspect of each of these types of fitness is important.

One aspect of physical fitness that is important is cardiorespiratory endurance. Basketball is a fast moving game and I must be able to get up and down the court quickly throughout the game. As a basketball team we play a fast break strategy where the purpose is to score a basket from a rebound or turnover before the opposition has time to set up a defence. My position is guard where, after receiving the ball, I have to dribble the ball up the court to initiate the play or to be involved normally as the playmaker. I am continually on the move and this requires a good level of CRE in order to carry out my role effectively. When possession is lost I need to get back to pick up my player or to retreat to my position in the zone defence. I play front player and again I am continually moving as part of the zone. This pattern of attack then defend goes on continuously throughout the game, putting high cardiorespiratory demands on me. Having an efficient CRE system will allow my heart and lungs to supply sufficient oxygen to the working muscles.

One aspect of skill related fitness that is important is agility. Agility requires a co-ordinated combination of speed and flexibility. As a guard I have to move my body quickly to get into positions where I can set up the play and dribble the ball up the court. I have to do this at speed and this will involve changing direction quickly to get past my marker and having the ability to change dribbling hands if necessary. This will involve running fast and adjusting my body shape to maintain control and not lose the ball. When defending I must be able to keep up with the player I am marking. To do this effectively you have to keep between your player and the basket and keep a low body position. Again you need to be agile to move with your opponent at speed and also be able to change direction if required. Hopefully this will force your opponent to make mistakes, lose the ball or

Physical Education
Higher 2005 (cont.)

3. (a) continued

prevent the player from making a pass or scoring. One aspect of mental fitness which is important in basketball is managing your emotions. Basketball is a hard, fast game where emotions can run high so it is very important to manage your emotions. This means being able to control my feelings in demanding situations, for example when the game is close or when my opponent is putting me under pressure when I am in control of the ball. You need to be able to focus on your role and what is expected from you. In basketball it is important to keep our shape as a team and function together; all it needs is for one player to lose control for problems to start to arise. Basketball is a physical game where players pick up fouls both as a result of contact and often disagreeing with the officials. Being able to manage your feelings will result in you lasting longer in a game and not disadvantaging your team, especially if a foul occurs caused by speaking out of turn to the officials. Finally, you may be playing in front of an audience so it is important not to be affected by noise or comments from them but remain fully focussed. This will help in maintaining a high level of skill required in my position.

(b) Choose two different methods of training that you have used (or have considered using) to develop one of the types of fitness discussed in part (a).
Discuss the merits that each method offers for the development of your performance in your chosen activity.

The type of fitness selected is physical and the two different methods of training selected are Fartlek training and circuit training.

The merits of Fartlek training are that it includes continuous running as well as short sprint bursts, which are important to me in basketball. When playing I need to be running up and down the court, whether it is dribbling the ball to set up a play or running back to defend. Also I need to be able to use short bursts of speed to get past my marker or set up a fast break. Fartlek training develops both types of fitness required whether it be aerobic (continuous running) or anaerobic (short speed endurance sprints). Therefore it is appropriate to the demands of my role in basketball. This training would not only improve my CRE but also my dribbling control. In order to do this I would do some jogging mixed with more continuous running and shuttle sprints with or without the ball.
Other merits include the fact that it is easy to plan and can be done indoors or outdoors and it can be varied to suit my requirements or other players' requirements depending on their roles.
The merits of circuit training are that I can base the training on my own requirements. Again, this could be either role-related, as a guard, or designed for general fitness requirements for basketball in general. In basketball, as a guard, I could base my circuit on physical aspects such as CRE, strength,

3. (b) continued

flexibility, speed and muscular endurance which are important and specific to me. This would be done using a multi-station of different exercises. This will develop the muscle groups which I use. Alternatively, I could base my entire circuit on one particular aspect of fitness, e.g. cardio respiratory, by doing a set of exercises based purely on this aspect, so the type of training can be easily adapted to suit my needs. This form of training can also be carried out indoors and requires a minimum of equipment which makes it easy to organise, carry out and to record results. Finally it is easy to progress and overload by increasing reps of each exercise or by decreasing rest intervals.

(c) With specific reference to one method of training discussed in part (b), explain the importance of progressively overloading your training. Give specific examples.

When carrying out circuit training it is important to apply certain principles to your programme. Progressive overload is one of these and is very important to performance development. Unless the body is subjected to a certain level of stress its condition is unlikely to improve. Overload must be progressive so you are gradually increasing the stress we place on our body. As you train, your body adjusts to your current fitness programme and in order for you to improve your fitness you must adapt your programme, otherwise you will not make any improvement in your fitness level. In order to improve I need to progressively overload my training so that I exercise at an increasingly higher level. When we progressively overload the body it adapts and gets used to the new stress and can cope with the new overload. This results in us becoming fitter. If we want to keep improving our performance in the training then we must again increase the overload. This can be done by increasing the intensity, frequency or duration of the training. By progressively overloading, the body adapts and can eventually cope with the new demands placed on it. I have carried out a multi-station circuit working on a group of exercises to work the major muscle groups used in basketball. I worked on each specific exercise for 30 seconds and rested for 30 seconds in the first two weeks. These exercises included press ups, sit ups, squat thrusts, step ups, shuttle sprints and stride jumps. In order to progressively overload I increased the work period in weeks three and four to 35 then 40 seconds, as well as reducing the recovery period to 25 then 20 seconds in the following sessions. This made sure I was putting my body under stress and getting fitter as the circuit became harder. Another method of progression was to increase the sessions from twice to three times per week or increase the number of circuits I was doing.

(d) Discuss the effects that your training had on your whole performance.

When I was playing games I noticed that I was able to sustain a higher and more consistent skill level for longer because of my improved CRE. I was able to maintain my performance for longer and the onset of fatigue in the game did not occur until much later

3. (d) continued

than it previously had. This meant that I played better for longer and that I was in better condition towards the end of the game. When attacking I noticed I was still managing to support my team mates when setting up the play either with the fast break or, if this broke down, by being available to pass or shoot even in the later stages of the game. I also felt I was more able to dribble past my opponent more and, because I felt fitter and was able to keep going for longer without feeling as tired, I felt more confident in myself. Also, when defending, I felt that I was able to stay with the player I was marking and was able to get back to defend quicker if we were playing zone defence. This led to more pressure on the opposition, forcing them into mistakes which often resulted in us regaining possession and allowing my team an opportunity to score. Finally, because I felt fitter, I was motivated and happier with my performance and this improved my self confidence and led to a better overall performance.

4. Choose an Activity.

(a) Discuss why it is important to ensure that fitness training is:

(i) **specific to the fitness demands of the activity;**

Your answer must demonstrate understanding of the relevant key concept knowledge and its application. This addresses the application of different types of fitness in the development of activity specific performance.
Your answer should show knowledge about the fitness demands of the activity. For example, in swimming, fitness demands include speed, endurance, strength, local muscular endurance, flexibility, CRE etc. By having training that is specific to an activity, an improvement in fitness will lead to an improvement in performance. Your answer could also relate to your previous level of fitness so that you can improve any type of fitness through training to improve strengths or minimise weaknesses you have in the activity. This also gives you the opportunity to set realistic goals.

(ii) **specific to the personal needs of the performer.**

Your answer should show knowledge about the fitness demands of the chosen activity that are specific to the individual. Training could be role-related in a game or specific to you as an individual, based on your strengths and weaknesses. This gives you a starting point to improve your performance and again allows you the chance to set personal targets to improve your level of fitness and your overall performance.

4. (b) With reference to the specific demands of the activity, describe the methods used to make observations, and record data, about your fitness for performance. Briefly describe the development needs that you identified.

Your answer must demonstrate relevant knowledge and include a description of methods selected to collect data. The methods selected will depend on the type of fitness selected and must be relevant for the activity selected.

For example in swimming:

Physical fitness
Pool based
Data recording sheets looking at split times for speed endurance, number of breaths for cardio respiratory endurance and number of strokes for local muscular endurance.
T5 swim test CRE.
Land based
sit and reach test for flexibility
Bleep test for CRE.
Skill related fitness
Pool based
Video looking at stroke for coordination of arms and legs, balance in the water or reaction time at starts.
Land based
Illinois agility run for agility.

Mental fitness
Questionnaire about your feelings during a race.

The development needs identified should relate to the activity and the fitness relevant to the activity. For example, when swimming the 100 metres front crawl I discovered that my split times on lengths three, four and five got considerably slower, showing I needed to improve my speed endurance. This was backed up by an increase in breath counts and by the bleep test done outside the pool where I managed an average score. My development needs were to decrease my split times and breath counts by improving my speed endurance and my level of CRE.

(c) Outline a programme of work you used to meet the needs you identified.

Your answer must demonstrate understanding of the relevant key concept knowledge and its application. This is planning, implementing and monitoring training in pursuit of personal goals.

The programme of work must relate to the activity as well as to the needs identified in part (b). For example, to improve my speed endurance and CRE I undertook fitness training in the pool, which is performance based. I trained four times per week with a rest day in between. The minimum time for my programme would be six weeks. Each session would have a warm up, then some drills followed by the main set to improve the fitness that needed to be improved. Within the answer there should be some description of the actual work done. Detail should also be given showing how the principles of training were applied to the training programme. For

Physical Education
Higher 2005 (cont.)

4. (c) continued

example, increase the number of reps in a set or decrease the rest period between sets.

(d) With reference to your whole performance, discuss the effectiveness of your programme of work.

Your answer must demonstrate an understanding of the relevant key concept knowledge and its application. This is planning, implementing and monitoring training in pursuit of personal goals.

The answer must relate to your whole performance. Examples could include:
- Improvement in my overall time
- Decrease in split times in comparison to previous
- Decrease in number of breath counts to previous
- More efficient stroke.

AREA 3: SKILLS AND TECHNIQUE

5. Choose one activity.

(a) Explain in detail, what you understand about the principles of effective practice when developing skill and/or refining technique.

Your answer should show knowledge of the relevant key concept and its application. This addresses the ways of learning skills and developing technique.

Your responses should reflect that practice methods selected for improvement should be specific to complexity of skill and relevant to your stage of learning. The acronym S.M.A.R.T.E.R. is useful for this purpose. For example, practice should be **s**pecific, **m**easurable, **a**ttainable, **r**ealistic, **t**ime related, **e**xciting and **r**egular. Other relevant knowledge will reference factors such as practice needs to show progression to ensure targets were reached/enabled refinement /remediation/regression as required, increased motivation, improved confidence, consideration of work rest ratio etc.

(b) Select a skill or technique. Discuss how you used data gathered and other information sources to plan your performance development.

Your answer should show knowledge of the relevant key concept and its application. This addresses skill/technique improvement through mechanical analysis, movement analysis or consideration of movement.

Include a brief description of methods used and offer relevant details of associated criteria. For example:
- Movement Analysis: (Observation checklist, Match Analysis sheet)
- Preparation/Action/Recovery: Mechanical Analysis of force, levers, propulsion etc
- Consideration of Quality: reflecting on whether your skill or technique was controlled/fluent, or fast/slow

5. (b) continued

- Video: Comparison of your performance with that of a model performer. The video allowed playback, freeze frame.
- Questionnaire: Questions should be relevant to and have responses such as 'done well', 'needs improvement' or you could mark your performance on a graded scale.

Evidence of logical and critical thinking must be evident when explaining how these methods were used to plan for improved performance. For example, I used video and an observation checklist to identify strengths and weaknesses and make comparisons before/during/after training. I used video and an observation checklist to ensure reliability/avoid human error. KU about how these helped in the selection of appropriate training methods must be evident. For example, I decided to use gradual build up, repetition practice, etc. On completion of my training I used the same data sources to compare/analyse if improvements had taken place.

(c) Describe, in detail, a programme of work you used to develop this skill or technique. Give examples of how the principles of practice were applied in the programme.

Your depth of response must be detailed and demonstrate critical thinking. You must show evidence of how the selected methods of practice featured as important aspects within your programme. This should be relevant to your identified skills or techniues/complexity of the task/stages of learning etc. As you offer detailed explanation about your programme you must show how you applied the principles of practice to ensure your programme was successful. For example, I made my problem-solving drills game-like so that I would be challenged and motivated to succeed... I made my practice harder by adding in more defenders.... I got immediate feedback on my performance so that I knew when I had improved... Once I had reached my target I would use more complex drills such as... to ensure I did not become bored I decided to... etc.

(d) On completion of your programme describe how your whole performance was affected. Outline what you would do to ensure your progress continued.

The depth of response will reflect upon the selected development of skill or technique. You must show critical thinking and offer evaluative comments about improved performance. This must be supported with relevant information about how your whole performance was affected. For example, on completion of my training I could see that I more consistently won games... The execution of my smash was much more fluent and had more power... I could now... etc. To ensure that my progress continued I would set higher targets by... I would continue to use pressure drills but add in ... I would compare my results and, if required, go back and further refine my technique by... etc.

6. **Choose one activity and a skill or technique.**

(a) **What information about your performance were you able to obtain using one of the following methods of analysis.**
   (i) **a mechanical analysis**
   (ii) **movement analysis**
   (iii) **consideration of quality**

In a gymnastics competition, I needed to perform 2 complex vaults to get graded. In practice I decided to use consideration of quality checklists to help me identify which of my vaults I performed most consistently.

These sheets contained specific questions about my technical competence when executing my vaults. Recorders filled these in using grading criteria of 1- 4; which ranged from excellent to poor. From this information I was able to identify important features about my vaults. Firstly I could examine the degree of difficulty of each vault (for example, the number of different parts it contained and which ones looked the most difficult and exciting to watch). I was also able to look at how competently I performed each of the vaults. I was able learn about the way I performed my run up, take off, flight phase and landings. Very importantly, I could judge the general aesthetic quality of the overall technique. This was important for me as judges in competitions will award high marks if the skill selected is complex and exciting to watch.

I performed my vaults several times to ensure reliability. I learned that my best 2 for competition purposes were my long arm over swing and the more complex one off hand spring with half-twist dismount. My performance in each of these vaults was recorded as excellent and very consistent. My run ups were powerful and fast when I took off, I had good height in my flight phase, which gave me the time to perform the technique before I landed. I consistently spotted my landings and looked in control. This was extremely important and so I decided to dedicate my practice sessions to working specifically on these 2 vaults. I used my checklists throughout so that I could get feedback from my coaches on any remaining weaknesses and fine tune my performance ready for my next competition. I would then be able to use these checklists during my practice sessions and refer to them to see if I was improving.

(b) **Describe, in detail, two different methods of practice you used to develop your performance of the skill or technique identified. Explain why you considered each of the practice methods selected to be appropriate.**

When developing my long arm over swing vault I decided to use repetition drills only. As this was the easier of my 2 vaults I knew as long as I took sufficient rest periods then repetition practice would be appropriate for me to work on perfecting my timing at take off from the trampette. Repetition of the 'whole' skill was much easier for me and was the quickest way to help me refine my technique. I was already comfortable with my performance and used these drills simply to make fine adjustments to

6. (b) **continued**

improve the overall aesthetic quality of my vault, for example extend my legs slightly earlier. This also allowed me to get immediate feedback from my coach. The actual vault takes seconds to perform and by repeating the action over and over again I became more confident and extremely consistent about all aspects of my performance; in particular my flight phase and my landings. The more I did the drill the better I got, I was then able to move the trampette slightly farther back to increase the complexity of the vault; it also made it more exciting to watch.

For my other vault (the hand spring with half-twist dismount) I used gradual build up practice. I did this because of the complexity of the vault. I was not at the automatic stage of this vault and had problems with my half-twist. To be honest, this had as much to do with my confidence as anything else. To ensure I made progress I would practice specific parts of the technique. I started performing the handspring on the floor. At this stage I worked on the power of my run up. I then added on the half-twist. With no height drop from the apparatus to worry about I was able to concentrate more and take in the feedback offered by my coach. I then used the box but not at full height, I used extra crash mats to ensure I was safe. I had mistimed my twist dismount a few times and hurt myself so I felt the need for these extra mats. Once I had worked on sorting out my take off from the trampette I was able to execute the movement with more height and so had more time in the air in which to perform the half-twist. I finally moved onto the full height box but initially left the extra crash mats to give me confidence. Once I felt more consistent and confident I took the extra mats away and repeatedly practised the whole vault. Both practices used were appropriate as they were specific to the complexity of the skill and matched my level of skill performance.

(c) **From the list below, select two of the factors that are influential in skill development. Discuss how each of the factors chosen affected the development of your skill or technique during practice.**
   • **motivation**
   • **feedback**
   • **anxiety**
   • **concentration**
   • **confidence**

The two factors that affected the development of my vaulting ability were feedback and confidence.

When practising my first vault I relied very much on kinaesthetic feedback. I was already comfortable with the skill and so could feel how well I was performing. I knew when my legs were not extended or whether I had managed to spot my landings accurately or not. I also received verbal and visual external feedback from my coach, which also helped me to improve the overall quality of my technique. As the feedback was immediate I was able to take on the advice given and put it back into my whole performance. This type of feedback was important but had more of an impact on me as I practised my second vault. This was because this vault was much harder to perform.

Physical Education
Higher 2005 (cont.)

6. (c) continued

There were more sub-sections involved and therefore I needed diagnostic feedback from my coach to enable me to refine specific parts of my vault. I also needed the feedback frequently as I was not consistent and made errors at different sections. Closely related to feedback was my confidence. Due to the danger element of performing vaults it was crucial to be confident in myself so that I would not tense up and mistime my run up or take off. I had to be confident in my 'spotters' who were there to prevent me from falling. The repetitive nature of my practice increased my confidence very quickly and so I was able to make my performance look very relaxed and easy to perform. The gradual build up process reinforced my inner confidence, the more feedback I got the more confident I became and the fear of falling became less of an issue. My confidence also affected the aesthetic impression of my vault in that when I was unafraid I was able to get much higher in my flight phase and could also rotate more quickly on my half-twist dismount. During competition my confidence had to be exceptionally positive so that I would not make mistakes. At this time although I was nervous because I was performing in front of a crowd, I had to ensure I believed in myself and so make my vaults look more spectacular and so gain higher points from the judges.

(d) Skilled performers are able to select and apply the right skill at the right time.
With reference to a skilled performance in an activity of your choice, discuss this statement.

As well as my vaulting I am also required to perform a floor work routine when competing. I have often used skilled performers as an incentive for me to make improvements in my own performance. I would love to make my performances as good as theirs. When executing their tumbling skills they make it look effortless and certainly do not seem to worry about the danger elements. They can perform a wide range of technical skills which means that their routines are breathtaking and very exciting to watch; many leave the crowds gasping at their endeavours of combining handsprings, baranis and front or back somersaults. Always, they look fluent, well controlled and totally relaxed in their manner. Good decision making skills are evident in their choreography as they select and combine simple and complex skills in time to music; almost as though it was always meant to be. I admire their expressive talents as they add head and arm gestures to make their routine unique. Although I try very hard to imitate these performers I have a long way to go and need to work on the execution of my complex skills and improve my choreography greatly if I am to improve upon my artistic impression.
They have high levels of physical, skill and mental fitness to help them maintain their form throughout. Most skills require high levels of power and flexibility to enable them to get height as they transfer body weight from one movement into

6. (d) continued

another. I think the best attribute a gymnast needs is balance. When you consider that at one instance the gymnast will have offered a fast tumbling sequence and the very next instance has to demonstrate total stability (e.g. maintain a handstand) this is what gets you high marks. They have tremendous powers of concentration and are able to block out distractions from the crowd. If they make a mistake they are able to disguise it immediately and help to reduce the damage of lost points.
All in all I feel I admire the fact that these performers rarely seem to make any mistakes. They keep well disciplined and work hard throughout all the required events to enable them to gain maximum marks. I also admire the fact that these performers are on their own: they do not have other team members to rely on. This for me makes it the greatest challenge.

AREA 4: STRUCTURES, STRATEGIES AND COMPOSITION

7. Choose an Activity.

(a) Explain why it is important to consider the demands of the performance situation before selecting a Structure, Strategy or Composition. Make reference to the factors you would consider.

Your answer should show knowledge of the relevant key concept and its application. This addresses identification of strengths and weaknesses in performance.
Answers should highlight the important factors that must be considered to ensure the best Structure, Strategy or Composition (SSC) is selected.

These could include:
- Strengths and weaknesses of your own team or opponents
- Particular strengths of individual players in your team
- Experience of previous results
- Experience within your team
- How long you can apply the SSC selected
- Score in the game
- When in the game to apply/adapt/change

(b) Describe, in detail, a Structure, Strategy or Composition that took into account at least one of the factors considered in part (a).

Your answer should show knowledge of the relevant key concept and its application. This addresses the structures, strategies and or/compositional elements that are fundamental to activities.

Answers should include a detailed description of SSC appropriate to selected activity. For example: we played a 2-1-2 zone defence against our opponents because we knew they were good at driving to the basket and we wanted to force them to shoot from outside the zone. We knew this from a previous game which we had played against them at the beginning of the season. We also had three tall players who formed a very good rebound triangle so we were able to collect the rebounds better if they missed their shot.

7. (c) **Describe circumstances that required you to adapt or change this Structure, Strategy or Composition. Outline the adaptations or changes you made, and explain how they ensured your performance remained effective.**

Your answer should show evidence of information processing, problem solving and decision making to develop and improve performance. Answers should have a description of the problem faced, what you did to adapt or change the performance and how it ensured effective performance.

For example: our 2-1-2 zone worked reasonably well but then one of the forwards of our opponents started shooting more baskets so we changed to a box and one zone where we put one of our front players in the zone to mark this player man for man and the other four players in the zone played a 2-2 to cover. This was effective because it put pressure on this player and did not allow him to score any unopposed baskets and at the same time the others could still play an effective zone.

(d) **Describe what you would do in the longer term to further improve your ability within the original Structure, Strategy or Composition.**

Your answer should show evidence of information processing, problem solving and decision making to develop and improve performance.

Answers should highlight the need to make refinements and adjustments to ensure even better application.

For example even though we knew that the SSC was vulnerable to good outside shooters we wanted to make it work and make it better so we continued with pressure and game-like drills to improve our movement out to the shooters and improve the specific role of the two guards at the front of the zone. This improved our team work and our defensive qualities and allowed us to become more consistent.

8. **Choose an activity.**

(a) **Select a Structure, Strategy or Composition. Describe the strengths a performer(s) requires to apply this Structure, Strategy or Composition effectively. For example, you may wish to consider the physical, technical and/or the mental strengths required.**

The strategy I have chosen is the fast break in basketball. As a team we need a variety of strengths. First of all I am going to describe the physical strengths we require as a team. When applying the fast break, players, especially the guards and forwards, require a high level of CRE as well as speed endurance to enable us to continue to sprint quickly down the court to allow us to score a basket before the opposition gets a chance to set up their defence. As we want to do this frequently during the game we need to have this high level of fitness. We also require certain players to have good strength to block out players and for jumping when rebounding both defensively and offensively. As the fast break can start from a rebound, it is important to gain the ball from the boards if the opposition misses their shot

8. (a) continued

defensively and equally as important that our centres need the strength to do the same offensively if we miss our shot.

Technical strengths are also required. Players need to have good techniques in particular skills to carry out the fast break well. These include ball handling, dribbling and passing. As a team, passing is very important, especially the outlet pass from the rebound etc. which starts off the fast break. This pass has to be fast and accurate as does the final pass to try to create an overload to the forward for a drive to the basket to score with a lay up. Ball handling is also very important with good technique required in catching the ball from the rebound and being able to control the ball when receiving the pass to shoot. This is important for all players in the team. Dribbling is important for the person who collects the first pass and then dribbles the ball down the middle of the court to the top of the key before releasing the final pass to one of the forwards to complete the fast break.

Finally, mental strengths are required. Players must be mentally strong and remain focused on their role within the fast break. Every person has a particular role to play and must fully concentrate and be alert in order to enable the strategy to be carried out effectively. One missed pass or lack of concentration can lead to a turnover which gives the opposition an opportunity to counter attack against you. The forward who receives the final pass really has to be determined to complete a successful lay up as they may be under pressure and because the final success will depend on them scoring.

(b) **When performing in the activity chosen, explain the importance of one of the following factors.**
   - **Group and team principles**
   - **Choreography and composition**
   - **Tactical and design elements**

I have chosen Group and team principles.

First of all, communication must be effective, especially when we are applying the fast break in basketball. The person who is receiving the first pass must let the rebounder or the person who has collected the turnover know that they want the ball. This should be a call for the pass. This will then enable the fast break to start effectively. Communication in all parts of the strategy is important so that players can receive the ball when they are free or in the best position to receive the ball. Also when playing basketball when defending, communication is important, especially if you are playing man to man defence where each player has a particular player to mark. If a player is having difficulty in marking or if they lose their player, they require help to prevent their marked player from scoring. By good communication, a team mate can respond to the call for help by coming across and marking that player. Supporting each other is also important. By doing this, players can create many options which will allow more opportunities to score, or give players under pressure a chance to pass or allow the team to keep possession of the ball. In the

Physical Education
Higher 2005 (cont.)

8. (b) continued

fast break, support is important. If the fast break cannot be carried out it is important that there are players who are able to support and set up an alternative option.

When playing basketball width, depth and mobility are important. In any play a team wants to be able to cover the width of the court as well as the depth of the playing area. Mobility must also be applied so that a team can adapt and change depending on the actions of the opposition. When attacking in basketball, width is created by the forwards staying out wide in the court hopefully trying to pull the opposition's defence out wide to create space behind them for other team mates to exploit. Alternatively they themselves can create depth and mobility by driving past their defender to the basket. Depth is important so the team are trying to get in behind the defence and allow forwards or centres to cut and drive to the basket and score from close in. Mobility is important because in any game the team will be faced with different situations that have to be overcome, either defensively or offensively. As a team it is important that you can change or adapt your strategy. For example, if we are playing half court man to man defence and you find you are committing too many fouls or the opposition are driving to the basket you may change to zone defence to restrict the space and force the opposition to shoot from outside rather than drive to basket.

(c) With reference to the Structure, Strategy or Composition selected in part (a), give specific examples of how the factor described in part (b) is applied to ensure an effective performance.

When applying the fast break we first of all made sure that the communication channels were effective. The person collecting the first pass always shouted clearly for the ball so the person who had the ball knew exactly where the ball was to go and this ensured the move got off to the perfect start and this would allow this person then to dribble down the middle of the court for the next pass. This also ensured a quick delivery of the ball which is crucial in the fast break.

We supported each other by getting up the court fast so that the person dribbling the ball down the middle had the option of passes to either side, so one player could then hopefully score a lay up. This would lead to an easy basket being scored. Also if the fast break broke down at the top of the key, we had players in place to change or adapt to another play which also is an example of mobility.

Width, depth and mobility were also applied to the fast break. At the start of the move we had two forwards out wide in the court to receive the first pass and after the person who had received the first pass had dribbled down the middle, the person who had initially started the break would sprint down the free lane. The person with the ball now had an option to pass left or right, again to one of the players out

8. (c) continued

wide who would receive the pass. The person with the ball now would drive to the basket showing depth and mobility in this attacking move.

Mobility is applied to the fast break by the options that we have as a team. If the defending team can stop the forward out wide at the top of the key then that forward can fake as if to shoot and reverse the ball back to the person at the top of the key who has meanwhile taken a step closer to the basket. This player now has an opportunity to jump shoot and hopefully score. Another option is for the guard dribbling the ball down the middle to pass the ball early to the forward out wide who can then pass the ball across the court for the other forward to drive to the basket and score.

(d) Describe a practice/practice session where you tried to develop your performance using the factor chosen in part (b).

To improve our communication we practised the first part of the fast break. We would work in groups of three where we had a person throw the ball on to the backboard and rebound the ball. Two forwards were positioned out wide opposite the top of the key. The forward at the side of the basket where the rebound occurred would then shout 'ball' and the rebounder would pass them the ball with a quick, accurate pass. The forward would then dribble down the middle of the court and the rebounder would fill in the free lane. We would continue and carry out the whole break with one of the forwards scoring a basket. This was repeated several times so that as a team we would be able to fine tune the part we were practicing but still carry out the complete strategy. This would be carried out unopposed to begin with as a 3v0. We would then introduce a passive defender and play 3v1. Later, active defenders who would put us under pressure were introduced. This ensured that we would be faced with a game-like situation and pressure as it is important that the practises are game related and should be relevant. At the end of the session we would play a full court game where we tried to use the fast break as much as possible trying to use the part we had practised.

Physical Education
Higher 2006

AREA 1: PERFORMANCE APPRECIATION

1. Choose an activity.

   (a) **Describe, in detail, the range of qualities you require to perform effectively in your chosen activity.**

   As a hooker in Rugby I feel I need a range of qualities to enable me to perform my role effectively. These qualities I feel are best described as technical, physical, mental and special qualities.

   I need a full repertoire of technical qualities such as the ability to catch, pass, tackle, kick etc. It is important that I am consistent when I apply these skills and do not give the ball up easily. Catching and passing need to be accurate especially in tight situations. Tackling has to be fierce and performed precisely to stop my opposite number from gaining yardage. Throughout the game kicking is an essential feature and one which has to be performed quickly as opponents try to close down your options.

   I need many physical qualities such as good cardio-respiratory and muscular endurance to help me work hard throughout the duration of the game. I certainly require good upper and lower body strength; in scrums this is essential as I am anchored between my prop forwards as we try to win the ball back from a put in. I also use my strength to dig into the ground to enable me to maintain my balance and so limit the space my opponents wish to exploit. In rucks and mauls strength is very much required as I push to help my team maintain or regain the ball.

   I need mental qualities such as controlling my anxiety to help me focus so I make less mistakes when under pressure. Rugby is an aggressive game and so controlling anxiety helps me not to react to the odd kick or punch that inevitably happens during the course of the game.

   Special qualities help for example, anticipating play and reading the game situation well helps me create attacking opportunities for my teammates out of nothing. For example, just by noticing a player in better space and releasing a pass to him quickly we can take territorial advantage.

   (b) **Discuss how two of these qualities described in part (a) affected your own performance.**

   I would say the two most important qualities were my technical and physical qualities.

   Although this might appear big headed, I know I have high levels of physical fitness and rarely tire during the game. I have good technical abilities so I produce a consistently effective performance. I have worked hard during training to ensure I am match fit and am confident in my ability.

   As a hooker I am technically gifted. I am a secure ball handler and therefore rarely give the ball away. My tackling is powerful and I always stop my opposite number from gaining yardage by knocking him quickly down to the ground. If I do not deck him, I delay him and make him lose his balance. When

1. **(b) continued**

   required I consistently put the ball into touch which gives us time to regroup. A very important part of my role is to throw an accurate ball in from a lineout; my timing has to be spot on as does my placement. I am able to vary the length, speed and height of the ball that I throw in; this gives us a good chance of retaining possession. When this happens we can immediately attack and take territorial advantage. My good physical qualities, such as high levels of cardio respiratory and muscular endurance help me to produce sustained effort in my tackling, rucking and mauling for the duration of the game. The nature of the game demands constant forward, backward and sideways movements. This is tiring enough but not near as exhausting as the low/high movements of getting back onto your feet when you have been brought to the ground. For example, having grounded my opponent I have to get up quickly and immediately take up position to support play. I know I contribute well in this department. I have very good upper and lower body strength; in scrums this is essential as I have to hold onto my prop forwards and hook the ball away from our opponents as we try to win the ball back from a put in.

   At the level I play rugby it is very aggressive and competitive. From previous game results, personal and coach feedback I know that I am consistent and play effectively in my role. This makes me confident and I am always in the starting fifteen. I am reliable in my defensive duties and always stick to our game plan, I believe in good teamwork and try to encourage my teammates as much as possible especially in scrum ball and lineout situations where communication is essential.

   (c) **Discuss the importance of long and short term goals. Give examples of the goals you set to improve your performance.**

   Importantly taking account of short term goals will enable me to work effectively to achieve my long term goals.

   Planning is crucial as I needed to think about what I wanted to achieve immediately, for example, maintaining my general fitness and consistency of my technical abilities and importantly stay injury free. This would have an impact on my training priorities for my long term goals to help our team win the league for a third consecutive year. This makes tremendous demands on me as an individual but the same demands are there for us as a team unit. The season is physically and mentally demanding therefore our preparation to achieve goals is crucial. As I have said our short term goals were to maintain general fitness, refine our technical abilities and win our weekly league matches. Our longer term goals were to develop more specific aspects of fitness and improve our tactical plans so that we would have more practiced alternatives when playing against our rivals.

   For example, short term goals were addressed by weekly training schedules; 3 times of 1 to 1 1/2 hours. In these sessions we worked on our fitness and skill maintenance by using a conditioning approach. Specific drills were used in the form of a 6 station

Physical Education
Higher 2006 (cont)

1. (c) continued

circuit aimed at improving role related duties of passing, tackling, kicking and line out throwing etc. These sessions finished off with the use of tackle bags in a 1v1 or 2v1 drives to help improve our defensive skills, this kept us motivated as it was game like and more challenging; mini games were also incorporated.

In the longer term, we planned to devote more time to our strategic play.

The league championship is usually a four team race. We have won the last two years but feel to ensure victory we need to improve our game plan and devise new tactics to give us the upper hand.

We had to be dedicated to team practice and work hard on both our fitness and skills and used repetitive practice of set plays to ensure application became automatic. At this time we relied heavily on video replay of previous performances to improve our tactics. We also reviewed the performances of our rivals so we could be ready when they presented us with challenges.

During this period our coach would experiment with players playing different roles so that we were all match fit and able to fulfil and or change roles at any time in the game, for example if we used substitutes. The incentive to win three in a row was the biggest goal we needed.

(d) How did you monitor your performance as you worked towards achieving your goals?

To be honest, monitoring was easy as it is a very important part of our preparation throughout the season.

During training our progress is monitored in various ways. For our short term goals, we used progress charts and record sheets of statistics of passing, line out successes etc. We then compared previous results which gave us an incentive i.e. we had to try and beat previous targets. During this period standard fitness tests were used to test specific areas related to cardio-respiratory , muscular endurance as well as speed and agility. Our coach would give us feedback and if required make us do extra training. The most reliable method of all was watching our league positioning which appeared in the local newspaper.

In the longer term we focused on our target of championship succession. Video replay was the most reliable and powerful tool. With our coach we would sit together and pinpoint weaknesses take this back onto the training field and rehearse improved moves. Training as well as match play was recorded with game statistics a very prominent feature of our discussion. Honesty being the best policy, we gave each other criticism when it was due. We knew each other well enough to accept it and used our own internal feedback to accept or reject points made. This proved to be right and as a result we tried even harder in practice the next week. The final way in which we monitored our progress was our parents who attended just about every game. They certainly told it like it was.

2. Choose an activity.

(a) Explain how mental factors can influence performance.

Your answer should demonstrate knowledge and understanding in relation to mental factors such as managing emotions/ levels of arousal; both cognitive and somatic, etc. Reference may also be made to internal factors affecting performance such as negative thoughts or lack of self confidence OR to the external factors affecting performance such as dealing with criticism from supporters etc.

Your answer must include critical thinking about how a positive or negative mental attitude can affect your performance. You should be knowledgeable about how these factors can make your performance better or worse and include specific examples. You may also include detail about the measures you could take to help you deal with controlling emotions / anxiety etc.

For example, a positive mental attitude helped me to remain focused during the game. This helped me to blot out external factors such as crowd shouting...

Handling arousal helped me to be determined and I responded well to the game challenges etc...

Having negative thoughts made me anxious. I was scared of my opponents and so I often made unforced errors. These thoughts reduced my confidence and I worried more about the mistakes I made instead of...

To stop these negative thoughts I used mental imagery by... I could see myself.... etc.

A good answer will reflect upon both the negative and the positive effects that this can have on your performance and offer detailed examples to support your answer.

(b) Model performers can cope well with the demands of performance. With reference to one specific demand compare your performance to that of the model performer.

Your answer will depend upon the specific demand selected. For example, when playing Basketball – taking a free throw at a crucial stage of the game.

Your answer should include a detailed description about how the model performer would react to the demands of the challenge and include details about how they would perform. For example, a model performer would not get flustered and would be in control showing good composure. The crowd would not upset the pre-setup routine... The model performer would be focused on the basket... The preparation action and recovery of the shot would be smooth controlled and accurate... The baskets would always be scored... etc.

You must then show critical analysis when comparing and contrasting your own performance. Explain the similarities and the differences.

For example: I got very nervous and fidgety.... I was not relaxed and my pre-set up routine was unbalanced... The crowd put me off... I did not take time at preparation stage my balance was poor and I rushed my shot... My follow-through was lacking in power which upset my aim and I often undershot hitting the rim... My accuracy was usually one out of two....etc.

2. continued

(c) **Discuss the course of action you would take to bring about an improvement in your performance.**

Your answer must demonstrate critical thinking and show knowledge and understanding about the specificity of the action you took. You must include specific examples of what you did.

For example: I selected to train using a whole part whole approach. By isolating and concentrating on specific sub-routines of my shot for this I used repetition drills to develop my free throw technique.... I included mental rehearsal as I shadowed the shot. This helped to... I then used several repetition drills... I practised in both closed and open situations to enable me to learn to handle the pressure... etc.

Your answer should also include details about how you progressed your practice to ensure improvement. For example, now that I could get 20/20 baskets I increased the number to 30... I decided to shoot a series of an initial 10 then 20 shots with my eyes closed, this improved my mental visionary of the shot going in and developed the rhythm of my technique. In our 3v3 training games random free throws were called to enable me to take the shot in more game like situations. This made me more confident and more accurate... etc.

(d) **Discuss the effectiveness of your course of action. Describe how your overall performance was influenced.**

Your answer must demonstrate critical thinking in relation to any improvements in your performance. You should make reference to your specific technique improvement as a result of your course of action and then discuss whole performance improvements. Give opinion about your course of action. For example, ...the repetition drills greatly improved my technique... successfully the drills I used made me more confident and helped me increase my overall success rate. Furthermore, my technique mirrored more the model performers... I took time in my pre-set up routine to make sure I was focused, my routine was consistent, I took an extra couple of seconds bounced the ball, took a deep breath and then released it high following through longer... I no longer was aware of opponents fidgeting at the key trying to put me off... I was inwardly confident, more relaxed and this improved my accuracy... etc. This affected my whole team performance, I had a lot of pressure on me at these times and I felt responsible for my team... because I was more accurate this increased their confidence too... although you cannot predict when in the game free throws will be awarded we were ready... my game statistics improved which helped my whole teams league status... etc.

AREA 2: PREPARATION OF THE BODY

3. **Choose an activity**

(a) **Describe in detail one method you used to assess your fitness in the chosen activity.**

Explain why this method was appropriate.

3. (a) continued

The activity I have chosen is swimming and my event is the 100 metre front crawl. The method I used to assess my fitness was to collect data about my performance on a recording sheet. On this sheet I had one of my classmates record times for each 20 metre length I completed and two other class mates also took data on my stroke counts and breath counts for each of the 5 lengths that I swam. We worked in groups of four and changed each time one person had completed their swim until all four of us had completed the task.

This method was appropriate as split times gave me information on speed endurance which is crucial to front crawl swimming. The stroke count gave me information on my muscular endurance and the breath counts gave me information on my CRE.

The information gathered was also specific to my performance in the pool so was valid, reliable and objective and tested aspects of fitness which are relevant to my performance in my stroke.

The method used also gave me information on my level of fitness so I was able to identify my strengths and weaknesses. From this I can set suitable training targets for me to work on.

Finally I could compare my times with a table of norms and others in the class which will act as an indication of my ability and also motivate me to do even better.

(b) **Select one method of training and say why this was appropriate. Describe in detail one training session using this method.**

The method of training I used was interval training which was carried out within the activity. This method of training involved me training for a particular period of time then resting and then working again.

This method of training is appropriate because it enables high intensity work to be carried out alternating with periods of rest giving the body time to recover. The high intensity work will ensure that my fitness level progresses and combined with the rest periods it will also allow me to train for a longer period of time allowing greater benefits from the training.

Interval training is also appropriate because it can work on a variety of aspects of fitness, for example it can be used to develop both aerobic and anaerobic fitness and therefore can be adapted from session to session. This could be done in a variety of ways for example the time or distance of each period of exercise or recovery between each period of exercise or sets and repetitions in each training session.

Interval training is easy to overload once my body has adapted to the training. This can be done by changing the number of reps in a set, the distance to swim, the rest period or the speed at which I swim.

One training session that I carried out was as follows: First of all I started with a warm up which was 8 lengths using a variety of strokes so that I was raising the body temperature and increasing the blood supply to the heart and preparing my body for the harder session ahead.

Physical Education
Higher 2006 (cont)

3. (b) continued

I then went and did some stroke improvement by working on the arm action by working with a pool buoy between my knees, trying to improve my arm pull to help greater pull through the water. I did 2 x 4 widths.

I then went on to my main set which consisted of 6 x 50 metre swim with a minute recovery between each. This was working on my speed and speed endurance where I was working for a short period with a longer rest in between.

I then did a sub set of 6 x 50 metre swim with a recovery period of 45 seconds. This was increasing the intensity of the swim by decreasing the rest period between each swim.

Finally I did a warm down which was 4 lengths slowly, looking to prevent any build up of lactic acid due to the intense session that I had carried out.

(c) Discuss why the principles of training are important when designing a training programme.

I first of all would set short and long term aims or goals. This would ensure that my training always had a focus and this would help to keep me motivated. It also would encourage me to regularly monitor my progress to make sure I was making some improvements and that my training was set at the correct level.

When designing a training programme there are many principles that are important. By applying certain principles it ensures that I can get the best from my programme. The first principle was to make sure that the training programme being designed was specific to my event and the demands of my event which were speed endurance, strength, muscular endurance and CRE. Specificity will also apply to my specific personal strengths, weaknesses and needs as identified in my data gathering. This should eventually lead to an improvement in my fitness for my event.

Unless the body is subjected to a certain level of stress then its condition is unlikely to improve. Specific demands must be applied for the training programme to be effective. Principles applied to make the programme harder are frequency, intensity, duration and rest and recovery. I worked three times per week with every other day a rest and recovery day. The body needs to rest to recover from a hard training session and will through a rest day be prepared for the next hard session.

I also made sure that my training programme would last for an appropriate length of time so I could improve my fitness and achieve the targets which I had set out at the start of the programme. The minimum amount of time would be 6 weeks, and I would be looking for nearer 12 depending on the aspects of fitness being addressed.

Intensity is important as I was improving my fitness for my event and as I was carrying out interval training, my training was at a high intensity so I

3. (c) continued

made sure that within each session my main and sub set were set to achieve this in terms of sets, reps and recovery periods.

I also had to make sure my training programme was progressive and that I applied the principle of overload. When we progressively overload the body it adapts and gets used to the new stress and can eventually cope with the new level of overload and become more efficient. If I want to keep improving my performance in my event then it is necessary to increase the level of overload that I would place on my body. This could be done in different ways depending on the particular aspect(s) of fitness that I am working on. For example if it was speed I would work faster than normal, or strength work the muscles harder than normal.

Throughout all the sessions I would ensure that there was variety within the drills to prevent boredom and keep my motivation high.

(d) Explain why it is important to evaluate the effects of your programme on your overall performance.

It is important to evaluate the effect that the training programme had on my whole performance so I could check whether the method of training and the content of my programme was correct. I found that I had a reasonable improvement in my fitness levels for my event. This could be seen by the improvement in my overall time for the 100 metres front crawl as well as a reduction in my split times, stroke counts and breath counts in comparison to my initial data collection. This was due to am improvement in the aspects of fitness that I was trying to improve.

I could also determine that my training programme had been set at the correct intensity and making sure I had not been over working.

I would also find out through evaluating my performance whether I had achieved the goals and targets that I had set out at the beginning of the programme. Since this was the case it gave me the motivation to try and improve my overall performance further.

It would also allow me to determine what still had to be worked upon and what I might require to do in the future now that I had completed the programme and seen the effects on my performance. I might now try to improve my technique through improving another aspect of fitness in flexibility.

4. Choose an activity

(a) Describe the fitness requirements needed to perform effectively in the chosen activity.

Your answer should demonstrate knowledge and understanding in relation to the types or aspects of fitness that are necessary for your performance to be effective in the activity you have chosen. This could be taken from all three types of fitness which are Physical, Skill related or Mental Fitness. You could also describe in detail one type of fitness and refer to some of the various aspects that are included in that type.

4. (a) continued

Your answer must show why the fitness selected is important to effective performance in the activity. You should try to relate your answer to the nature and demands of the activity.

For example, in football I play as a centre midfield and I need to have excellent cardio-respiratory endurance. This is an aspect of physical fitness. I need to support both attacking and defensive players in my team at various stages throughout the game and this requires me to be constantly on the go. If I do not have a good level of CRE then I will find it difficult to sustain this supporting role for the entire 90 minutes in a game. Also my skills may deteriorate towards the end of the game which will not only affect my performance but also that of my team. Strength is also required in football to win the ball in tackles... This allowed my team to regain possession and set up more attacks, creating an opportunity to score. It is also important in holding players off when you have possession of the ball. This meant I could retain the ball etc.

A good answer will describe the fitness requirements and give detailed examples to show the effectiveness when they are used in a performance.

(b) The training year can be divided into 3 phases or periods.

- **Preparation or pre-season**
- **Competition or in season**
- **Transition or off season**

Select one phase or period. Describe in detail the content of a training programme you used to develop a specific type of fitness during this phase or period.

Your answer must show knowledge and understanding in relation to the type of fitness selected and its relevance to the phase or period selected not just the content of a training programme of the fitness selected.

For example: I have selected the pre-season phase and have planned my programme to be ready for the start of the new football season... I was working on building up my CRE by running long slow distance runs twice per week lasting for 20 minutes at a time. Having a rest day in between... always trying to stay within my training zone... increased this to three times... still rest day in between... Final two weeks increased to 30 minutes per run. I then went on to do some more demanding aerobic work in the form of a circuit training programme specific to both my role and football in general. It concentrated on both skill related and physical fitness, e.g. squat thrusts, bench jumps, press ups for physical fitness and short passing and moving practices, dribbling and tackling for skill related fitness.

I used a heart monitor to show I was always in my training zone.

In the competition period you would have already developed a strong CRE base and would possibly carry out a conditioning approach where your training within the activity to peak for particular competitions... fine tuning your preparation... I used

4. (b) continued

interval training... working at a high intensity... 3 sets of 6 reps with a 1:3 work rest ratio... variety of exercises... I also worked on practising and fine tuning particular movements like free kicks and corners routines which we use as a team.

In the off-season time it was important to keep a level of general fitness. I would work at a low intensity, mainly on aerobic work and general running... take part in other activities to maintain general aerobic fitness (could include swimming, cycling, football etc).

(c) Discuss the importance of planning to help implement and manage your training programme.

Your answer must show critical thinking about the planning and management of a training programme. For example it is important for your training programme to have a particular aim. I set myself specific goals, both short term and long term. This gave me something to work towards. The goals had to be realistic and achievable. This motivated me to do well. My short term goal was to improve my overall performance in football by being more consistent in games. I made sure that my training still dealt with refining my strengths as well as developing my weaknesses.

I made sure my programme was challenging but achievable and relevant to my ability. I used specific principles of training to ensure progression. Each session had a warm up, main focus and balanced activity. This made training enjoyable. Improvement and success motivated me to do well. I monitored the programme before making adjustments. All of these points are important when planning and managing your programme.

(d) Discuss the effectiveness of your training programme on your overall performance. Give examples of your future development needs.

You must demonstrate critical thinking in relation to any improvements made in your performance. This must relate to your whole performance.

For example: in my midfield role in football... Over a period of time my training significantly improved my performance. I was able to last longer in a game... The onset of fatigue did not occur until later and I played better for longer and was in better condition at end of a game. I gave up less often as I had a better level of CRE. I was able to support the attack more often and get back in defence to help out... I also won more tackles by pressurising my opponent more than before. All of this made me more confident on the ball.

Your future development needs must be relevant and realistic.

For example: I want to try and improve my speed so when I win the ball on tackles I can get away from the player quicker and set up team mates... Or improve my strength to hold up the ball for my team mates.

Physical Education
Higher 2006 (cont)

AREA 3: SKILLS AND TECHNIQUE

5. Choose one activity and a skill or technique.

(a) Explain the benefits of considering a model performer when learning or developing this skill or technique.

Regardless of the activity chosen or skill or technique selected your depth of response must be detailed and demonstrate critical thinking by offering good examples to support your answer. You should explain the importance and the benefits that model performers can bring to your developmental process. You should consider some of the following important features in your explanation:

• Identifies your strengths and weaknesses
• Increases your confidence, motivation
• Provides you with various types of feedback; qualitative, quantitive, diagnostic etc.
• Provides you with challenge in practice/ competition
• Provides you with accurate feeds continuously
• Can inspire you to achieve higher levels of achievement
• Enables you to plan practice/set targets appropriately
• Enables you to copy ideas

For example: I watched model performers in my class. I was inspired by them and wanted to be as good as they were. When perfecting my left hand lay-up I got feedback from them and they provided me with 1v1 challenge. I loved this level of direct competition and used this as a form of target setting; this kept me motivated and determined to do better. I gained in confidence and felt that my technique had greatly improved as a result... etc.

(b) Describe briefly, how you gathered data/information about your performance in this selected skill or technique. Give specific details of how your performance compared to that of a model/skilled performance.

You must demonstrate good knowledge and understanding about the data/information sources used.
The data/information sources used should reflect the type of skill or technique you have selected. Depending on the data/information sources used you should include a brief description and offer relevant details of associated criteria, for e.g.– Movement Analysis (Obs. c/list) – P.A.R. Mechanical Analysis– force, levers, propulsion etc, Consideration of Quality – controlled/fluent, fast/slow etc. Video – Compare v split screen, rewind/review etc. Questionnaire – Questions relevant to direct response of done well; needs improvement or grade of 1–5 etc.

Evidence of logical and critical thinking must be evident when comparing your performance to that of the model performer.
For example: When playing basketball, I used video and Obs. C/L to identify my strengths and

5. (b) continued

weaknesses and make comparisons to a model performer competent in the left hand lay-up shot I used video and Obs. C/L to ensure reliability/avoid human error... This also gave me instant feedback and I could see compared to the model performer that I was not fluent in my movement, I looked clumsy in the air.... I noticed that I failed to take off at the correct time and was not balanced when in the air.... I also noted that... etc. You should give as many examples of good/weak features of your skill/technique as possible to gain full marks.

(c) In relation to your current performance, describe in detail a programme of work that would be appropriate to develop the skill or technique identified.

Your depth of response must be detailed and show knowledge of why the programme of work selected was appropriate. The programme selected should be relevant to your identified S or T/complexity of the task/S of L, etc. As you offer detailed explanation about your programme you must show how you applied the principles of practice to ensure your programme was successful. The acronym S.M.A.R.T.E.R. is useful for this purpose. For example, practice should be specific, measurable, attainable, realistic, time related, exciting and regular. Other relevant knowledge will reference factors such as practice needs to show progression to ensure targets were reached/enabled refinement/remediation/ regression as required, increased motivation, improved confidence, consideration of work rest ratio etc.
For example: Compared to the model performer I was at the associative stage of learning and so decided to initially use shadow and repetition drills. This helped me to get the feel and a high degree of success before moving onto...
As my confidence and skill level increased I moved on from the 'closed' repetition practice and made my practice more challenging by first adding in a passive defender... then an active defender. I also included problem solving drills so that I would be challenged and motivated to succeed... I made my practice harder by adding in more mini games... I got immediate feedback on my performance which helped reinforce what I should be doing... I set realistic targets and once I had reached my target I would use more complex drills such as... to ensure I did not become bored I decided to....etc.

(d) Explain why it is important to monitor the effectiveness of your programme of work.

Your depth of response must be detailed and demonstrate critical thinking by offering good examples to support your answer. You should explain why the monitoring is an important part of the developmental process.
You should consider some of the following important features in your explanation:

• Ensures both short and long term targets have been reached.
• Ensures the programme of work is effective.

5. (d) continued

- Enables progression/regression as required.
- Enables change/adaptations to be made
- Promotes motivation and challenge

For example, monitoring my practice period was important. Not only was this motivating but it provided me with detailed feedback about my technique development... During my programme of work I was able to change my initial targets to ensure that my progress continued I would set higher targets by... I would know when to adapt my programme and added more pressure drills to make sure I was applying my lay up in game situations... but add in... I would compare my results and if required go back and further refine my technique by... etc.

Your answer must demonstrate related KU and critical thinking in relation how you used different methods to evaluate the effectiveness of your programme.

For example, on completion of my practice programme, I evaluated how effective it was by making comparisons about my game performance and percentage shooting rate. I compared these current match statistics to my initial performance... I also used the video and found this to be the most appropriate in terms of motivation and simplicity to use... The video captured the action as it happened, thus avoiding human error... After reviewing the video I was able to evaluate the quality and control of my flick shot and make qualitative judgements... I was able to back this up from the supportive data contained in my match analysis sheets by examining the quantitative evidence... I also relied on my own opinion about the improvements I made in terms of accurate shots against number of attempts made and whether or not I had reached my personal short and long term goals... if I had made improvements then I judged that the programme I had set up was pitched at the correct level for me.

6. Choose an activity.

(a) From your experience in this activity, describe a complex skill or technique you have attempted to develop. Explain why you found this skill or technique difficult to perform.

In badminton, a complex skill I found difficult to perform was my cross court drop shot. The reason I found this so difficult was because of the demands of execution phase of the shot. The precision required to play this shot was extremely high; requiring disguise but at the same time speed to ensure my placement was spot on so that I could wrong foot my opponent. Any error in any phase of the execution of the shot upset the flight trajectory. Often I played the shot too high over the net. This was heavily punished by my opponent who came in early and played a quick net kill. Another difficulty I had if I failed to time this shot properly was that because one side of my court was totally exposed it restricted my ability to get back into position early enough to defend. This shot is played from mid or rear court. It can be played from both my forehand and backhand side; the backhand being the harder of the two.

6. (a) continued

The preparation phase is the same as the clear, weight on the back foot, racket up, focus early on shuttle, on the action phase, my weight is transferred forward with the hitting action made at the peak of the height, I make sure my racket head is angled as I draw down across the shuttle to ensure a tight net drop is delivered onto my opponents side. On recovery I quickly push off my right foot to get balanced to move quickly back to the T position ready and anticipating the next shot.

My technique is not too bad but my weakness is the consistency of my delivery. I am aware that I usually hit it too high so in my attempts to get a tight net angle I can sometimes under hit my shot causing it to hit the tape and unfortunately drop on my side of the net. Played consistently however it is a great shot to have in the armory.

(b) Describe, in detail, two different methods of practice you used and considered important to develop this skill or technique.

When developing my cross court drop shot I decided to use repetition and combination drills to develop my technique and shot placement.

Repetition of the shot I felt was the quickest way to help me refine my technique as I could get consistent feedback and accurate shuttle feeds from my partner who is the same standard as me.

The nature of these drills helped me make fine adjustments to improve my technique; mainly the timing in my follow-through and racket head angle, and also develop good footwork and anticipation. The other good thing about these type of drills were that I could get my partner to vary the type of feed. By varying the height, speed and direction of the shuttle I was making sure that I could adapt to any game pressure. I was able to set targets and progress once my targets had been reached. For example, sometimes I would concentrate on straight drops only to get my confidence and timing going then I would move onto the more difficult cross court shot. I could easily adapt my practice by using hoops. Videoing or taking statistics was also possible. During the pick up of the shuttles before starting another repetition drill I was able to practice some shadow hits of the drop shot. This allowed me to refine my shot as I could catch my reflection on the window and watch myself shadow the shot; I used this as feedback. More importantly because I was not under game pressure I could do as many as I liked without worrying about my next shot.

After rest periods I would move onto combination drills. These were important due to game like pressure. Not only did these drills help me to execute the cross drop shot more realistically but I was able to develop other parts of my game such as fitness and mental focus. With my partner we would start the rally with a high serve then overhead clear, then drop shot then net shot then underarm lift and repeat to start the rally again. Although I knew the sequence of the shots to be played the nature of these drills allowed me to play a greater range of shots so forcing me to be accurate whilst refining my footwork and court coverage. The other advantage of using these

Physical Education
Higher 2006 (cont)

6. (b) continued

drills is that if more rest periods are required they could be added in. The degree of difficulty could be increased to make me work harder for example, two net shots before lifting etc.

This also allowed us to give each other immediate feedback. I was fortunate in that my partner and I play regularly and are of the same standard. This is important because these drills need a high degree of precision and so feed placement is essential otherwise the rally breaks down. These drills forced me to deal with the challenges I would face when playing full court singles.

(c) Explain in detail, the principles you took into account when using these methods of practice to ensure your performance was effective.

I took the principles of effective practice into account when using both my repetition and combination drills. Knowing how to apply certain principles made sure I progressed for the standard I played at. For example, the specificity of the drills I selected was correct for my level of play. It was important that my partner and I could feed accurately to each other; otherwise the rally would break down. We were both at the automatic stage of performance and so the specific nature of repetition and combination was appropriate for us allowing us time to get feedback and take sufficient rest periods. Importantly we found them challenging which kept us motivated and determined to do well. We were able to play competitive games at the end of the session to see if specific weaknesses were improving; for me this was the drop shot, for my partner this was the net shot. When using the drills we knew to progress the complexity of the drill to ensure further progress. For example, in the repetition drills we would increase the number of consecutive feeds and target ourselves to reach 10 then 15, 20 and so on. We would then feed randomly i.e. to different areas of the court, sometimes 2, 3, or 4 to the back hand side and then either the same number or different to the forehand side. This would make to nature of the practice more unpredictable. Getting feedback was good even if on occasions this would feature as a comment to each other such as "good well done", "great shot" this kept us motivated. In closed practice of the repetition drill targets were placed on the court see diagram below:

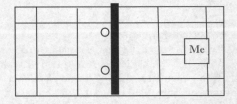

From where I am on court I am required to place my return drop shot into the hoop. I would increase my target number once successful.

6. (c) continued

Making targets meant that we were able to measure our improvements quantifiably. Moving onto combination drills ensured even greater progress due to the game like pressures we incorporated.

Once competent with the initial sequence we would adapt this, for example, instead of moving back from the underarm lift we would on occasions add in 2/3 net shots before lifting, similarly we could play a random number of overhead clears before executing the drop shot; this refined the disguise of the shot. To motivate us even more we would award ourselves two points instead of one for an outright winner of the drop when used in the practice games used to finish our drill training. The good thing about all our drill training meant that we also had the advantage of regressing a stage if we were unsuccessful at the current stage. Feedback remained high as we constantly able to tell each other why things were not working. Equally important was my own feedback, not only could I feel the action of the shot and feel instinctively that it was good or bad I could see the number of shots I played into the hoop. We ensured our practice remained effective by maintaining competitive challenge.

(d) Having developed your skill or technique in practice, discuss why your performance may still not be effective when applying this skill or technique during whole performance.

I often think about 'does practice make perfect?' Sometimes I wonder why I put all the hard work in during training. I feel in practice once warmed up and ready that I am totally in control, confident and it often feels as though I could never make a mistake. I play a full repertoire of shots accurately and feel I place my shots consistently and rarely make mistakes. This feeling of confidence is strong and I rely on it in that even if I do make a mistake I can quickly get over it and not let it bother me. My court coverage is efficient and I move smoothly into the ready position in anticipation of the next shot. In match play however I am under different pressures. I still have internal factors to deal with such as my confidence, handling arousal etc, but I also have to cope with many external factors affecting performance. For example, my parents often come to watch me play; although I find this encouraging as I know they are proud of me, this can sometimes make me nervous. Also the type of competition gets to me; I am naturally competitive and always want to give of my best. When playing at top level I do not have to worry about my fitness as I know I will last punishing rallies, less effective however is the consistency of my shots when the match is tight. If under extreme pressure my attacking play can let me down. A few mistakes on my cross court drop shots and I find that I have to defend furiously. Instead of getting the angle of my shot tight to the net I play it too high and am punished or my disguise is non existent and so my opponent can anticipate my intent. This upsets my rhythm and concentration and can find I lose 3 to 4 points in quick succession. I know that in practice I am much more relaxed and

6. (d) continued

confident and will need to learn to handle competitive pressure much better than I am doing if I want to make it to the top.

AREA 4: STRUCTURES, STRATEGIES AND COMPOSITION

7. Choose an activity

(a) Describe in detail a Structure, Strategy or Composition you have used. Outline the role you performed when applying this Structure, Strategy or Composition.

The strategy I have used is in basketball and is the fast break. The purpose is to try and score a quick basket and catch the opposition defence out. This can start from various situations. It can start from a turnover by our team when defending our basket, a rebound from a missed shot by the opposition or after a basket is scored by our opposition.

My team usually run it from a rebound or after a basket; we look to start the play with an outlet pass made out wide to a player at the side of our key away from the opposition. Communication between the person passing and receiving the ball is crucial. The player who has received the pass now dribbles the ball down the centre of the court until they reach the top of the opposition key, meanwhile the person who started the break and the opposite forward run down each side of the court out wide to fill the lanes and get ahead of the dribbler. Once at the top of the key the person with the ball now decides which forward or person to pass the ball to. The ball is now passed to one of these wide players who have filled the lanes and will now hopefully have an unopposed drive to the basket and will be able to score with a lay up. The other forward should continue to the basket and try to rebound the lay up should it be missed. My role was that I was the guard who was to receive the ball from the rebounder or first passer and then dribble down the middle and then pass the ball to one of the wide players so the fast break got off to the correct start.

(b) When performing your role within this Structure, Strategy or Composition, discuss some of the decisions you had to make during your performance to ensure that you carried out your role effectively.

As the player responsible for receiving the ball from the rebounder or the first passer I had to make sure was in the correct position to receive the ball, this was out wide and that there was no opportunity for that pass to be intercepted by the opposition as I was still close to my own basket and any pass intercepted would lead to the opposition having an opportunity to score. I also had to make sure that I communicated with the person passing the ball so they knew that I was in the correct position to receive the ball from them. This would enable the fast break to get off to a good start.

Once I had received the ball I then dribbled the ball down the middle off the court and then was faced

7. (b) continued

with the next decision of passing the ball. Often as I reached the top of the opponents key I would be faced with an opponent and I had to make sure that I drew them towards me and then passed the ball to one of my team mates who hopefully had filled the wide channels and then this would allow them an easy lay up and a chance to score a basket. It was crucial do to this as the timing of this pass will determine often the final outcome of the fast break. A bad pass may delay the break and cut down on the opportunity to score or allow the opposition a chance to get back and defend. Worse still an interception could lead to a counter attack by the opposition and we would be struggling to get back in time to defend as we had three players committed up the court. Again with this pass I had to decide which forward to pass the ball to as I had a choice and sometimes I could take the decision to go alone if I was faced with no defenders.

(c) Describe the method(s) you used to gather information about your role when applying this Structure, Strategy or Composition.

In order to gather information about my role I got my coach to video our performance when we were applying the fast break and I used this in conjunction with data gathering sheets. The data gathering sheets were specific to my role as a guard and had criteria which I could judge my performance against.

The criteria consisted of me being in the correct position to receive the ball, communication with the first passer, dribble down the middle, the drawing out of opponent and finally the success of the final pass to the player out wide. This was filled in by myself after watching the video later. If it was successful a tick was applied to the correct criteria and if was not successful a cross was applied where it broke down. There was also a comment box to say why it was not successful e.g. pass behind forward wide or pass intercepted etc. This could then be assessed to see how effectively I was carrying out my role and would give me and the rest of my team useful information on aspects of the fast break and how effective it was carried out.

Finally, I also received verbal feedback from my coach at the end of the match on my overall performance as a guard.

(d) With reference to the information collected, describe a future development need and explain how this would improve your future performance.

As the person who is responsible for bringing the ball up the court I would like to improve my dribbling ability with my left hand. As I am right handed I tend to favour dribbling with my right hand which I am very confident with. At the moment I can dribble the ball reasonably well with my left hand but I would like to do this quicker and with more control. As I need to dribble the ball quickly to get up the court I would like to be able to dribble the ball confidently and quickly with either hand.

In a game situation I can receive the ball on any side of the court and a defender will very quickly work out which hand you favour to dribble with and may

Physical Education
Higher 2006 (cont)

7. (d) continued

try to push you on to your weaker side if they get the opportunity. If I am competent with either hand I will feel more confident on the ball whether I am on either side of the court. My role is crucial in the fast break and it is essential that I am comfortable dribbling the ball with either hand at speed.
If I can quickly get down the court through a fast effective dribble down the middle then there is every chance that the fast break will be being successful. If I lose the ball we could lose a basket or if I am slow at dribbling with my left hand the defence may get back quickly or the nearest defender may put me under pressure which will result in the fast break being unable to operate.

8   Choose an activity.

(a) Select a Structure, Strategy or Composition you have used. Explain the benefits that can be gained from applying this Structure, Strategy or Composition.

Your answer must demonstrate knowledge and understanding of the Structure, Strategy or Composition you have selected. You must not only describe the benefits but give specific examples of how these affect the chosen Structure, Strategy or Composition.
Your answer should give a detailed description of the benefit with an explanation as to why it is effective. For example, in football my team played a 3-5-2 formation... One benefit is the dominant midfield because of the numbers there and it is very mobile when applying... This is because we have two wide players who can support the attack when necessary and they can also track back to help out in defence as well... This also makes it easier to cover the wide areas... We also have more attacking options as one of the midfield players plays just off the front two strikers to support them as well as the wide players when necessary... This means more opportunities to score... It is easier to dominate midfield as we have 5 players closing down the opposition putting pressure on them... This forced mistakes and allowed us to cut down their attacking options.

(b) Explain the limitations that have to be taken into account when applying this Structure, Strategy or Composition.

Your answer must demonstrate knowledge and understanding of the Structure, Strategy or Composition you have selected. You must not only describe the limitations but give specific examples of how these affect the chosen Structure, Strategy or Composition.
For example: one limitation when applying the 3-5-2 is that when long passes are played by the opposition from defence straight to attack the defence can be exposed and attackers can exploit gaps to create goal scoring opportunities... This can be especially wide in defence where there is limited cover... Or, depending

8. (b) continued

on how the back three are situated, down the middle as there may only be one defender covering that area... Sometimes as well because we have 5 in midfield there can be a lack of movement due to the numbers there and we can be less creative than we would like to be as this area is crowded and less space is available.

(c) Describe a performance situation that required you to adapt or change this Structure, Strategy or Composition. Explain why the adaptations/changes were necessary.

Your answer must demonstrate critical thinking and show knowledge and understanding about the specificity of the action you took. You must clearly describe the situation which caused the alteration of tactics or formations. This should show what was not working in your Structure, Strategy or Composition or what the opposition were doing to make your Structure, Strategy or Composition ineffective.
For example: we played against a team who were playing 3-4-3 against us and were able to bypass our midfield by hitting long balls over the top... Their three forwards were able to latch on to these balls... And, as one forward in particular was very quick, he was able to get away from our defensive three and create goal scoring opportunities... Also their three forwards were interchanging all the time, pulling our defence all over the field... As we were man marking this caused gaps to appear for the opposition to exploit.
We changed our formation to a 4-4-2 so that we had an extra defender at the back... We took one of our 5 man midfield out to play at the back... This meant we could man mark the three opposition forwards... and prevent them creating as much opportunities to score. We also were able to play a sweeper as the spare defender... They were able to pick up any player who managed to get away from their marker... It now gave our defence depth and we were able to deal with the long direct ball over the top, which was one of the problems identified... It also meant we had 4 defenders to their 3 attackers.

(d) Describe how you evaluated the effectiveness of the changes/changes you made. Discuss the effects had on your overall performance.

Your answer should have description of what methods you used to evaluate the changes and also demonstrate critical thinking in relation to the effects on your whole performance.
For example: I used a match analysis sheet where I was able to gather data... This gave me information on how many times the attackers got away from defenders... how many tackles we now made... how many shots on target the opposition made, etc. You could also use video linked to observation schedules or written comments from your teacher or coach. I compared them to previous data to see if improvements had happened because of the changes. The effect on the overall performance was that by having a sweeper in operation when an attacker broke free from his marker, the sweeper was then in a

8. (d) continued

position to tackle or prevent the attacker from bearing in on goal unopposed... This led to fewer shots on target and more pressure on the attackers... Also we were now able to deal with the long ball over the midfield because we had an extra defender in place... So prevent the fast attackers from having a clear path to goal... Finally, by having four players across the back we were able to deal better and defend across the width of the park... This made crosses more difficult for the opposition as we were spread out and were able to close the players down more quickly.

Physical Education
Higher 2007

The presentation of answers in this booklet is as follows for the 2007 paper. Four model answers have been written, one in each of the main Areas of the course (Performance Appreciation; Preparation of the Body; Skills and Technique; and Structures, Strategies and Composition). These model answers have been written by experienced teachers of PE and cover the most popular questions tackled in the exam. They should give you an indication of how you could write your own answers about your own activities.

The remaining 2007 exam questions have short marking instructions. These are similar to the notes given to the examiners who mark the Higher PE exam. They focus on what should feature in a good answer. Remember though that these are only notes to guide you and should not be taken as an indication of the length of your answers in the final exam.

In the following, KU = Knowledge and Understanding

AREA 1: PERFORMANCE APPRECIATION

1. **Choose an activity.**

   (a) **Describe the nature and demands of a quality performance.**

   I play hockey for my school team and the nature of the game makes it quite exciting. It is a directly competitive game with two teams of 11v11; plus subs to roll on in the event of injury or change of tactics. The object of the game is to score more goals than the other team. The game lasts 70 mins with 35 mins each half. There are a number of rules to make sure players play fairly. All players need to accept the decisions of the referee if they commit a foul and play as hard as they can. Good conduct and discipline is expected. The game is played outdoors and so the weather and state of competition may affect the players and the end result.

   The demands of hockey are really challenging. All players have attacking and defending duties this places pressure on the players to play well. There are physical, technical, mental and tactical demands. If I give you an example from each you will see what I mean.

   The physical demands are high, players need high levels of cardio- respiratory endurance and speed endurance to enable them to fulfil both their attacking and defending roles. They must be able to sprint into position to receive / intercept passes or track back to deny their opponents space and time on the ball and last for the duration of the 70 mins. They need good power and strength to hit the ball far and take challenges when fighting for possession. The technical demands of dribbling, passing, shooting and tackling must be of a high and consistent standard to expose opponents' weaknesses. Players need to respond to these demands constantly

Physical Education
Higher 2007 (cont)

1. (a) continued

applying their skills with split second timing. The mental demands are like many team games where players must be well disciplined and in control of their emotions. This makes sure they are focused and do not give away silly fouls or passes. The concentration levels must be high so that the players cooperate and communicate with each other especially when under pressure. The type of competition played, whether a cup final or a practice game, will require different levels of mental control. The tactical demands are high with players having to cooperate and respond to the immediate game problem. In any given situation tactics will be used to gain benefits of width and depth and so control the tempo of the game. Rehearsed in practice, players should automatically know when to switch and adapt play to gain territorial advantage and win the game. Knowing about these demands helps you to cope with game pressures and are needed for a quality performance.

(b) Mental factors can influence your performance. Explain how you were able to manage your emotions and mental state for a performance in your selected activity.

I know that mental factors can have either a positive or negative impact on my performance.

I am going to talk about situations where my mental state had a negative effect on my performance. Usually before playing in important matches versus our rivals I get uptight and suffer from somatic anxiety. Somatic anxiety is when my body responds to a worrying situation for example, sweaty palms, butterflies in stomach etc. My job is to score goals and link with my teammates to pressure our opponents. Even before the game starts i.e. in the changing rooms, I start to worry about how I will play. I get panicky and have negative thoughts and my confidence goes down. I can feel myself breathing faster and hope that I will not let myself or the team down. Once on the pitch I seem to take ages to settle down. During the many 1v1 scenarios I am involved in I often let these negative thoughts interrupt my concentration; it is at this point that I often rush my passes or my movements into the D. My positioning is not well timed and I waste valuable scoring opportunities. This definitely upsets my rhythm and tempo when attempting shots at goal. I also find that this lack of control of my emotions affects my decisions and I make more unforced errors.

In preparation for these return matches I wanted to have a positive mental state to help me to control my emotions. I knew that if I practiced self control during my training then I would be able to combat my nerves and so deal with pressure situations; especially the 1v1 challenges and take control of the game by settling down a lot quicker. I used self talk and visualization, this helped me to focus and blot out the actions of my opponent etc. By repeating 'key words' to myself and imagining such things as

1. (b) continued

dodging past my opponent and getting into open space this not only raised my confidence but improved the consistency in my attacking play.

(c) When planning for performance improvement, discuss why it is important to use integrated training (combination) approach to develop your whole performance. Give examples from your training programme to support your answer.

By using an integrated approach to my training I am able to deal with two or more parts of my performance at once.

This is a good way to approach training as it can save time and often makes it more enjoyable as it develops more game-like situations. The nature of the hockey relies on team effort and so practising with your teammates builds up co-operation and tactical awareness. It provides good opportunities for feedback and lets me practise longer on some parts. It also allows players of similar role responsibilities to split off and practise their specific parts before joining back up again to give competition.

For example, in training I practised my technical skills using repetition and game related drills. This also helped me develop my other qualities at the same time such as my timing, movement and anticipation of when to move, cut into space, deny my opponents and support play. For example, repetition plays of set pieces such as a corner or free hits allowed me to practise my movement in relation to speed of the pass. In game related drills I worked continuously with little rest periods therefore I developed my skill related aspects of fitness whilst controlling the ball and handling my emotions when under pressure. A good example of this was when creating an overload situation in a defending drill i.e. 2v4 or 2v3 sharpens my reaction speed, movement to deny space and helps me to make the correct decisions. I have to control my aggression play hard but make sure I do not make contact with my opponent.

This integrated approach is also good because I can vary the opponents, position of delivery, type of pass in, etc, for example, receiving/defending the ball from the left and right, or when marking faster and stronger players than I am.

During training it is easy to adapt and progress as practices can be made more challenging if and when required.

I really like training like this because it is not as boring as running round a track on your own or as easy as just simply dribbling round cones to make your technique better.

I find my performance is more consistent and I adapt more quickly to the unexpected events that happen in a full 11v11.

(d) Discuss why it is important to monitor and review your performance development.

I know that it is very important to do both.

Monitoring I think is very, very important as this is happening all the time. During my training I always monitored how I was doing. I found that this kept me motivated and it provided immediate feedback. I challenged myself during training and took a note of the things I was doing better and noticed the things I

1. (d) continued

could still improve upon. If I found I was not reaching my targets I moved them. For example, if I found that my games related drills were too easy then I could make them harder. Monitoring also let me see how I was doing compared to my teammates, for example in the set pieces I was able to see if my timing and movement to passes was getting better. Monitoring during training is quick as you are constantly noticing differences in the things you can do better and if you are not getting better then that is the signal to tell you that you are either not working hard enough or that your training is not pitched at the right level.

On completion of my training this is where reviewing helped. This is the process that is best done at the end as it lets me compare first performances to my most current. I would be able to check if the training had worked. Had I reached my long term goals? Was I able to perform my skills better? Had I contributed more to my team strategies? Reviewing my training let me judge whether or not to continue my training on the same aspects or whether to move and address other weaknesses. Reviewing is also necessary as it let me evaluate whether the type of training I used worked and motivated me to select it again.

2. Choose an activity.

(a) Discuss the positive and negative influence of mental factors on performance.

Your answer must demonstrate related knowledge and understanding and critical thinking about how a positive or negative mental attitude can affect your performance. You should demonstrate understanding in relation to mental factors such as managing emotions/ levels of arousal; both cognitive and somatic, etc. You should be knowledgeable about how these factors can make your performance better or worse and include specific examples. For example, having a positive mental approach to performance will help you before/during performance. In this respect you may find that you are

- Well prepared, relaxed and confident
- Successful in your selection and application of skills and techniques
- Successful in handling pressure and rarely make mistakes
- Excited and looking forward to performing in competitive situations
- Positive and enjoy the challenge

On the other hand, having a negative mental approach to performance may influence you before/during performance. In this respect you may find that you are

- Anxious, unsure and unconfident
- Hesitant in your selection and application of skills and techniques
- Nervous when handling pressure and are more likely to make mistakes
- Full of self doubts and do not handle pressures

For example, a positive mental attitude helped me to stay calm and think about my responsibilities during the game….. this helped me to blot out external

2. (a) continued

factors such as crowd shouting ….. handling arousal helped me to be determined and I responded well to the game challenges etc..

Having negative thoughts made me anxious, I was scared of my opponents even before I went onto the pitch… I often made unforced errors and let my team down…. These thoughts reduced my confidence and I worried more about the mistakes I made instead of… etc…..

(b) Technical, physical, personal and special qualities are important when performing. Select three of these qualities and explain their importance.

Your answer must demonstrate related knowledge and understanding about how 3 out of the 4 qualities offered are important to your performance.

For example, a range of different technical, physical and personal qualities helps me to play effectively in my role…. Having these qualities enables me to perform a wide range of technical skills physically well whilst remaining focused on our team strategy…etc

If you include Technical qualities you may consider some or all of the following points

- wide repertoire of skills
- consistent selection and application of skills
- accurate with high success rate
- proficient in both attack/defence (if referring to a team game)

If you include Physical qualities you may consider some or all of the following points

- strength
- speed / speed endurance
- muscular endurance
- cardio- respiratory endurance
- flexibility
- power

If you include Personal qualities you may consider some or all of the following points

- competitive
- control of temper / emotions
- motivated
- determined
- focused

on the ball, space, positioning of my opponents and teammates as this helps me to make the right decisions during the game. I am also fearless when it comes to tackling.

If you include Special qualities you may consider some or all of the following points

- select and apply skills with flair
- can fake intent
- create opportunities/ space / time
- disguise placement

Your answer should include a detailed description about how the qualities help you to perform effectively in your selected activity.

(c) Describe, in detail, the strengths and weaknesses in your whole performance in relation to one of the qualities you selected in part (b).

Your answer should demonstrate knowledge and understanding in relation to your specific strengths

Physical Education
Higher 2007 (cont)

2. (c) continued

and weaknesses. Your answer must also include critical thinking and show a link to one of the qualities previously talked about in part (b).
For example, the technical strengths I have as a wing defence in netball relate to my ball handling, intercepting and distributing passes. I believe I am consistent in these departments and this helps.... etc. However I believe my man to man marking could be better, I often fail to block space from my opponent and so they get away from me too easily...etc. You should include as much detail as possible.

(d) Explain how you organised your training to improve your weaknesses whilst maintaining your strengths. Give examples from your training to support your answer.

For example, I selected to train using a whole part whole approach. By isolating and concentrating on better footwork I found that I could improve my blocking... etc I used repetition drills to develop my footwork, this involved dodging marking and throwing practice. I would always be the marker and 'boxed' the attacker to where I wanted her to go...etc.... helped to. I practised in both closed and open situations to enable me to learn to handle the pressure and gave me experience of playing against players of different abilities....etc

Your answer should also include details about how you progressed your practice to ensure improvement. For example, my initial target would be to intercept 6/10 feeds... I increased the number to 8 and counted tips and 3 second rule infringements as one of my successes.... I decided to practise at sideline situations which were easier to control once successful I moved more onto the pressure repetitions of practising centre passes ....This made me more confident and more consistent and also let me apply my other skills in context .... etc

AREA 2 PREPARATION OF THE BODY

3. Choose an activity

(a) Describe in detail the range of fitness requirements for effective performance.
Your answer should demonstrate acquired and applied knowledge of the fitness requirements that are necessary for effective performance in the chosen activity.

This could be taken from all three types of fitness which are Physical, Skill related or Mental fitness. Try to relate your answer to the nature and the demands of the activity.
For example in basketball I play the role of centre and I must have good strength so I can rebound the ball both offensively and defensively and also be able to block out my opponents when going to rebound in defence. This relates to physical fitness........in skill related fitness I must have good timing to jump when rebounding the ball so I am catching it at the highest point.......and in mental fitness I must have control

3. (a) continued

over managing my emotions as if I get annoyed or lose my focus I could pick up fouls and end up being fouled out of the game.
You could also select one type of fitness and describe in detail all the relevant aspects of fitness that are important for effective performance.
For example physical fitness. In basketball CRE is important as it is a fast game and you want to be able to keep attacking and get back in defence.........flexibility is important as you want to be able to change direction when dribbling.......strength is important as you need to be able to block out opponents when rebounding......speed is important as you need to get down the court quickly in the fast break.......

(b) Discuss why it is important to gather information about your fitness

Your answer should show knowledge as to why it is important to gather information on your fitness. For example it gives you information on your strengths and weaknesses in either the types or aspects of fitness that are important in your activity.......this lets you know what you require to work on in your training programme......gives you a bench mark to work from........helps set you realistic targets for fitness improvement either short or long term.....you can compare yourself to national norms........gives you a level to compare your results to after you have carried out your training programme and then allows you to see if your training has been effective ....gives you information on your fitness level and needs

(c) Training can take place:
• Within the activity (conditioning)
• Outwith the activity
• Through a combination of both.
Select one of the above and briefly describe a training programme. Discuss why it was appropriate for you to train using the selected approach

You must show both acquired and applied knowledge of the training approach selected.
For example in basketball within the activity I did a variety of practices involving skills and fitness.....these were dribbling in and out of cones to improve my skill of dribbling with different hands......also improve agility......short shuttle runs to improve my speed.......continuous running to improve my CRE......throwing the ball against the board and catching it to improve my rebounding within a time restriction...improve my timing of my jump.....

This approach was appropriate as it developed both my skills in a game as well as developing the specific fitness requirements in basketball.........it also allowed me to practise specific movements like rebounding which I use in a game......can be similar to the pressure demands in a game.....was easy to set up ...was fun and enjoyable... was able to be organised within a basketball court...

For example in basketball outwith the activity I went to a fitness room and carried out a circuit ....this was group of exercises which were based on the aspects of

3. (c) continued

fitness required for basketball.....I carried this out twice per week ....did sets and reps ...press ups for strength in arms and shoulders for rebounding........shuttle runs for speed........stretching for flexibility .....bench astride jumps for CRE .....

This approach was appropriate as it ....developed specific muscle groups......as well as general fitness and muscle groups..........it was simple to carry out.....it required the minimum of equipment.......it gave me variety in my training........it was easy to apply the principles of training ...gain improvement

For example in basketball through a combination of both I carried out a programme including specific drills.......including passing, dribbling and shooting improving not only my skills but some fitness aspects as well......I also did some fartlek training outside including short sprints..... and continuous running to build up certain aspects of fitness I needed to improve on. This was appropriate as it also improved my skills in the game.......also my fitness requirements......gave me variety in my training......kept me motivated and prevented boredom........and allowed me to practise specific movements similar to game situations

(d) Having monitored your level of fitness during your training programme you will have made changes. Explain why these changes were necessary. Give examples to support your answer.

Your answer must give explanations as to why your training was changed giving relevant examples of these changes.

Changes were made to my programme because I had found that the training was not demanding........I had reached a plateau ....needed to make training harder.....I had achieved my short term goal.......my performance had stayed at the same level........I wanted to apply the principles of training .... apply overload.....I wanted to achieve my long term goals......I was becoming bored with training....I wanted to make progress in my performance. Some of the changes were to...increase training from 2 to 3 times per week.......increase the amount of running in terms of distance......reduce the recovery periods between circuits from 1 minute to 45 seconds.....increase the number of sets of exercises I carried out from 3 to 4 .....increase the intensity I worked at......increase the length of time I trained for from 30 to 45 minutes per session.

4. Choose an activity

(a) Select an aspect of skill related fitness. Describe one method of gathering information on this aspect. Explain why this method was appropriate.

The aspect of skill related fitness I have chosen is agility which is important in badminton. The method I used to gather information on agility was the Illinois Agility Test. This involved me running round a set course of cones placed on the games hall floor and I had to complete the course as fast as possible. I

4. (a) continued

started by lying face down on the floor and when my partner shouted "Go" I had to run as fast as possible round the set out course. This involved me running at speed and having to change direction and turn as well. The cones were placed in such a way that I had to run round some and in and out of others. My partner took my time at the end of the course. I had three attempts with a suitable rest between each test and took an average of the three runs. I then compared my results against National norms for my age and sex.

This method was appropriate because it was a recognised National test for agility and I could compare my score against the National norms for my age and sex. I was also able to gain valuable information on my agility which was an important aspect of fitness in badminton. The results gave me a permanent record of my performance and gave me evidence to compare my performance to after I had carried out a fitness training programme to see whether or mot my programme had been effective. Finally the movements in the actual test were similar to the movements which I would do in a badminton game.

(b) Explain the importance of mental fitness within an activity ofyour choice.

The activity I have chosen is gymnastics. Mental fitness is important in gymnastics as I want to be able to perform at my best. When I am competing in gymnastics I have a set routine on the floor which I am expected to carry out to the best of my ability. I want to remain focused and calm and block out any distractions that may happen for example the crowd encouraging other competitors or other events going on at the same time I am performing. It is therefore essential that I can fully concentrate on my routine and manage my emotions. My floor routine involves many different skills and movements so it is important for me beforehand to rehearse my routine in my mind and try to envisage me carrying this out successfully. It is important therefore that I am positive and calm beforehand. If I am fully focused I will carry out my routine better. Confidence is important as I want to be able carry out the routine successfully as if I am not confident I am liable to make mistakes which ultimately will lead to a poor performance and affect my score in that part of the competition. This in turn will make me anxious and affect my emotions making me feel despondent.

(c) Discuss the importance of setting goals to improve your level of physical fitness. Give examples of the goals you set.

It is important to set goals so I can improve my current level of performance. I have discovered that my physical fitness is poor especially my CRE and speed endurance. At the latter stages of a basketball game I am struggling to get back and defend my opponent and this means either they get an opportunity to score more easily or another of my team mates has to help out until I get back in defence One of my goals therefore is to improve my CRE and speed endurance allowing me to get back in defence quicker so my opponent scores less baskets especially

Physical Education
Higher 2007 (cont)

4. (c) continued

in the later stages of the game. I would also like to be able to get up the court quickly and be able to score baskets and collect rebounds for my team as I play centre and that is my main function.

I tested my CRE fitness by carrying out the bleep test and my score was average for my age group set against the National norms. My short term goal was to carry out a training programme to improve my CRE and when retesting myself to have improved my score and achieved the next category. My long term goal was to reach the top category for my age.

Goals can be short term or long term and they give you a target to work towards. It is important that the goals I set are realistic and can be achieved otherwise this will lead to disappointment. Setting goals will let me see if my training programme is working and is effective. Short term goals can let me monitor my training and then allow me to judge when I can got on to reach my long term goals. It also allows me to keep focused and motivated to improve my overall performance. Achieving a short term goal motivates you, keeps you interested and then makes you determined to go on and achieve your long term goal. Setting goals allows me to record progress on my fitness and gives me an incentive to work hard and not only improve my physical fitness but also my overall performance. Games are often won and lost in the last few minutes and if I can score baskets and collect rebounds for my team at that stage because of achieving my goals then all the effort and training would have been worthwhile.

(d) Discuss how you planned and implemented a training programme to achieve the goals set in part (c).

When I was planning my training programme I made sure that my programme was based on various principles and factors. I had identified my weaknesses in physical fitness by carrying out a series of fitness tests so that was my starting point. I then set myself both short and long term goals to achieve when carrying out my programme. I also considered what particular type of training was most beneficial for me to carry out.

I made sure that my programme was based on the demands of the activity as well as developing my own strengths and weaknesses. I also made sure that my programme was specific to me and my role within the game of basketball.

I wanted to improve my weaknesses in my physical fitness which were my CRE and my speed endurance but I also wanted to make sure that my skills were also being developed so I decided on a conditioning approach so I would be working on not only improving my fitness but also maintaining my skills required for my role within the game.

I made sure that my training programme was challenging for me and achievable so I would not get bored but keep motivated to achieve both my short term and long term goals. Within my programme I applied the principles of training to ensure progression.

4. (d) continued

I planned my programme over an 8 week period and I trained twice per week during my PE lessons. Each session lasted 1 hour. The session started with a warm up and then a main focus which was a circuit to improve not only my physical fitness but my technical abilities as well. In the circuit I included a group of exercises to improve my CRE and speed endurance as well as maintaining general fitness for basketball. I also had exercises to improve specific skills like dribbling shooting and especially rebounding. As basketball is a competitive game involving more than one person I also did practices similar to game situations. These included game related drills, small sided games and set plays. I made sure that the practices were set at the right challenge level and had appropriate rest levels to get feedback. It was also important to vary the drills to avoid fatigue and boredom. At the end of each session I would play short sided then full sided games.

After 4 weeks I monitored my performance and retested myself to see if I had improved my performance in the bleep test and achieved my short term goal. This I had achieved so I applied progression and overload to my programme. I decreased the time between each circuit I completed so my rest period was slightly shorter and in my circuit I increased the number of exercises I completed in each set.

AREA 3: SKILLS AND TECHNIQUE

5. Choose an activity and a skill or technique.

(a) When learning or developing a skill, it is important to work through the three stages of learning. These are
- The preparation/cognitive stage
- The practice/associative stage
- The automatic/autonomous stage

Explain what you understand about each stage.

At the automatic stage (autonomous stage) performance looks skilled, controlled and fluent. There is a feeling of having plenty of time when applying skills with a high degree of consistency. A full range of skills to meet performance demands are apparent with a high level of decision making used throughout performance.

The depth of your answer must offer sound description with full detail and exhibit detailed KU about relevant features related to each of the three stages of learning.

You should consider some of the following important features in your explanation:

In relation to the preparation/cognitive stage - I know that there is
- Limited understanding of how skill/technique is performed
- The need for consistent use of various types of feedback (mainly external) to ensure success/learning/development
- Inconsistent application of the skill/technique- performance is just recognisable
- A very poor level of decision making when applying skills in whole performance.

5. (a) continued

- Little control, consistency or accuracy with movement patterns often looking clumsy

For example, when learning a handstand I often fell over....... I needed support from my partner to maintain my balance..... When performing my sequence I rarely put it in ... I looked awkward and lacked confidence... etc.

In relation to the practice/associative stage- I know that there is

- A good understanding of how skill/technique is performed
- There is still a need for various types of feedback (external/internal) to ensure success/learning/development but the performer uses and can rely more on kinaesthetic /internal feedback
- A more consistent application of the skill/technique- performance is more recognizable
- Some good decision making apparent when applying skills in whole performance
- More control and accuracy with movement patterns often looking more controlled; less mistakes being made

For example, When performing a handstand I fell over less often .... I managed without support from my partner but usually only one of my legs was high and straight..... When performing my sequence I put it in ... I looked good sometimes and was more confident about moving into another move....etc.

In relation to The automatic/ autonomous stage- I know that there is

- A very clear understanding of how skill/technique is performed
- Less need for external feedback to ensure success/learning/development and the performer uses and can rely more on kinaesthetic/internal feedback /self correct performance
- A consistent application of the skill/technique/few errors high success rate
- A high level of decision making evident throughout performance.
- A controlled, effortless and accurate set of movement patterns

For example, When performing a handstand I was consistent and could stay steady for at least 3secs .... I managed it effortlessly with both legs straight and toes pointed..... When performing my sequence I used it several times... I looked excellent and well balanced .. I usually linked it to another move for example, into a forward roll or bridge.

(b) Discuss why it is important to use different methods of practice at two different stages of learning. Give examples from your programme of work to support your answer.
Your answer must demonstrate related KU and critical thinking about the importance of considering and then selecting the most appropriate methods of practice relevant to the stages of learning selected.
For example, when learning how to perform my handstand when I was at the cognitive I knew to use gradual build up method of practice. This helped

5. (b) continued

because I was new to the skill....etc. When confident using the wall for support I moved onto trying it with my partner supporting my legs, this helped and gave me confidence... I needed plenty of feedback and this was provided by my partner.....etc.
For example, I knew at the associative stage I would need to use a lot of repetition sets to make sure I got more familiar and consistent at keeping my balance for longer .... I knew that I would get bored if practised too long so I included other skills as well... when confident I knew to progress the degree of difficulty by....etc.
For example, at the automatic stage I varied between repetition and combination practice... the repetition practice improved my timing and aesthetic quality of my handstand because I could hold it for longer ... I was also able to rely more instinctively on my own feedback during these practice sessions... etc the combination practice could only be used when I had a high degree of consistency and needed to link my handstand to take me into or out of another action such as a forward roll or bridge etc....

(c) Describe how you monitored your progress as you worked through your development programme.
Your answer must demonstrate related KU and critical thinking in relation how you used different methods to monitor your progress throughout your development.
For example, on completion of my practice programme I evaluated how effective my handstand was by making comparisons via partner feedback... I compared my current routine to my initial performance....I also used the video and found this to be the most appropriate in terms of motivation and simplicity to use... The video captured the action as it happened, thus avoiding human error.... After reviewing the video I was able to evaluate the quality and control of my handstand and examined the precision via qualitative judgments ..... I was able to back this up from the supportive data contained in my observation sheets by examining the consideration of quality criteria. ... I also relied on my own opinion about the improvements I made in terms of how long I held my balance and how easily I linked into both simple and complex skills such as forward rolls or rotate to face the opposite direction; this being quite complex...As I had set myself personal short and long term goals, I could evaluate whether my programme was set at the correct level for me.

(d) Having developed this skill/ technique, discuss the effect that this had on your whole performance.
Your answer must demonstrate critical thinking about how your improved skill level benefited your whole performance.
For example, I had a much more polished routine. I looked more in control and my legs were much more extended. Having more balance in my handstand gave me more time in my transition from one move into the other. .... My whole routine had more creative moves as I was able to use my handstand to vary tempo and direction... I also gained more points from

Physical Education
Higher 2007 (cont)

5. (d) continued

the judges as I performed my floor routine…. I could also perform better on the apparatus as I could …. My confidence increased and I found that I could maintain balance longer enabling me to walk on my hands whilst in control…etc

6. Choose an activity and a skill or technique.

(a) Describe the features of a skilled performance in this activity.

In rugby, I believe a skilled performance relates to applying a wide range of technical, physical skills whilst controlling emotions and dealing with competitive pressures. Applying technical skills allows players to perform their role effectively whilst contributing to the teams strategy. There will be consistent execution of related skills; such as passing, catching, tackling etc, with control, accuracy and precision. The skilled performance will look effortless with the notion of plenty of time to select and apply skills to meet immediate game problems, for example, responding and adapting to opponents' moves and decisions.

In a skilled performance, players will possess the required physical skills specifically; high levels of cardio-respiratory endurance to enable them to cope with continuous movements on and off the ball for the duration of the game, speed when keeping up with and closing down opponents, muscular endurance- especially in the legs required for explosive jumping to win line outs and dynamic power when involved in rucks and mauls, upper body strength when delaying opponents' movements. In a skilled performance players will also display good reaction speed and anticipation to make effective tackles and to start off attacks as opportunities present themselves at lightning speed.

Importantly, players will demonstrate total control of their emotions and be ready to capitalise on mistakes made by opponents. A very aggressive contact sport there are many on and off the ball clashes that require players to be disciplined so that penalties and 'sin bin' offences do not happen often. Concentration and focus is high to enable all players to work as a unit.

In a skilled performance all these features should be evident and maintained for the duration of the game.

(b) When learning or developing a skill or technique, discuss the importance of one of the following:
- **Information Processing**
- **Skill Classification**

I know that information processing involves reaction to a stimulus i.e. the brain sends a message to the muscles to ensure action takes place. The brain makes sense of the action taken and the whole process starts

6. (b) continued

again. This diagram shows how it works.

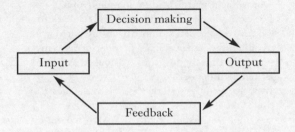

I know when I am learning skills that this process happens extremely quickly with all 4 parts linked together. At the input stage it is important that I pay great attention as this is when I receive information (known as stimulus or cue); this could be an instruction from my coach or movement by my team-mate/opponent. Secondly, based on this information I must make sense of this i.e. take on board what I have been told or seen and make a decision about what action I am going to make. Thirdly, at the output stage i.e. I need to respond to the information given and produce 'an action'. The last part is extremely important as this is where I receive feedback on how effective my action/decision was, for example, did I execute the skill appropriately? – based on this outcome the whole process starts again instantaneously. This feedback can be given externally/internally and often a combination of both. I have learned that this is a continuous process and the more experienced you are the better you are at it. It takes lots of practice to develop and good performers can do it automatically. Information processing relies on the person's ability to take in information and act on it as they get better they need less external feedback and can more accurately act upon on internal feedback when learning skills. Previous experience and complexity of the skill counts for a lot because at different times you may need to rely more heavily on instruction or demonstration before you are successful in learning and then able to apply the skill.

(c) Describe, in detail, the methods you used to gather information on your level of performance. Explain why these methods were appropriate.

The data methods I used included the video, match analysis sheets and specific questionnaire sheet.
I wanted to find out how effectively I was in my role as a hooker in rugby. Specifically, I wanted to know if I performed my defending and attacking duties consistently throughout the game. I decided to use the video as this was the best tool of analysis to avoid human error. The game is fast paced and I did not want to miss anything. The video allowed me to look at my game several times which let me check my match analysis and questionnaire sheets to see if they backed up what I was seeing. I could also discuss with my teammates and coach afterwards and get their expert opinions.
The match analysis was time related and divided into five minute sections for each half. I asked my marker

6. (c) continued

to indicate the number of passes I made or intercepted, the number of tackles I made, the number of times I forced my opponent to the ground and to count the scrum support that I offered, etc. My questionnaire was designed specifically to evaluate my mental skill. The specificity of the questions related to my success rate at controlling my temper; especially after making unforced errors or when the score was tight.

All these methods were appropriate as I was able to look at my strengths and weaknesses in my performance. Also I could discuss with my coach ways I could improve for example, I could then use this feedback to set targets for improvements. Using these methods were appropriate as I could compare my performance in the future once I had practised. I also found them to be very motivating and easy to use. The close angle viewing of my scrummaging meant that I could refine my technique and try harder to perfect it. As I had used more than one method and gathered information from a variety of sources I felt that my information was reliable.

(d) From the information gathered, briefly describe a programme of work you used to develop this skill or technique. Explain why it is important to review your programme.

I used this information to help me design a training programme that would effectively help me develop my defending skills. I decided to focus on my tackling. I used a series of repetition and game related drills. This helped me to develop both my technical skills as well as my general fitness at the same time. I felt it was essential that I practised under game conditions to produce a more consistent performance. In role related drills such as holding up my props in scrums and tackling I made sure I worked under pressure; this improved my anticipation to deny space, reduce time and options for my opponents. This also heightened my awareness to move earlier and tackle my opponents by body charging at worst and bringing them to ground at best. For example, my coach told me to be more aggressive when bringing my opponent to ground; in this situation my opponent can often 'kick out' to get free from me, instead of reacting back I learned to remain focused and made greater effort to get to my feet and get on with play.

The pressure drills of 'give and go' and 'box' practice with and without the use of tackle bags, were completed at various speeds. This again improved my anticipation and timing as I had to consider more than one cue at a time, for example, players were cutting into space sometimes 'open' sometimes 'marked', I was forced to consider options and make appropriate decisions. This was completed 3-5 times with a rest period in between.

I used repetition plays of 'put ins' at scrums and 'line outs', this again forced me to practise my reaction time and anticipation in relation to the ball, the immediate situation and positioning of my team mates and the opposition. This helped sharpen my reaction speed, reinforced my accuracy and helped me to make better decisions. These plays were repeated 5 times, first without opponents then with, to

6. (d) continued

make it game like- I learned to respond to the 'unexpected' situations. I would then finish off with small sided games to put my practice into the real thing.

It was important to review my training so that I knew if I was making improvements and achieving targets. It also gave me an opportunity to think about varying the order of the drills used so that I did not get bored and had a greater challenge. It allowed me to compare to previous performances and kept me motivated to do better. It presents an opportunity for reflecting on what still needs to be done as I believe you can always find ways of improving your game further.

7. Choose an activity and a Structure, Strategy or Composition.

(a) Discuss why it is important to gather information about your performance when applying the Structure, Strategy or Composition. Give examples of the strengths and weaknesses you found.

Your answer should demonstrate knowledge of the importance of gathering information. My activity is tennis and my Strategy is serve and volley.

For example I gathered information on my strengths and weaknesses to find out the effectiveness of my Strategy when playing .... The Strategy was based around my strengths .....so it was important to have knowledge to see if they were being maximised to full advantage..... and to see if my weaknesses were causing me problems........ the information allowed me to see where it was going wrong..........this allowed me to then plan a programme of work to help me improve the Strategy and use it more effectively........ it also gave me information whether I needed to change my Strategy..........it also allows me to see my opponents weaknesses....... it gives me information to pinpoint parts that were really effective......whether my strategy is suited to my particular needs.

The information I gathered told me ....I had a consistent first serve......it is fast and powerful.....and had a good percentage of being in......I often can vary the placement to my opponent...........I follow in quick after the serve.......my volley technique for my forehand is good.....I often make winners from my first volley. My weaknesses were my backhand volley technique is poor.......I make most errors from this volley...... usually hitting it out of court......or into the net......my second serve is weak.......often it is too short in length.....my opponents exploit this.....my percentage of winners from this is poor.

(b) Describe how you addressed the weaknesses highlighted in part (a). Explain the actions you took.

Your answer must demonstrate critical thinking and show knowledge and understanding about the action you took.

I carried out a programme of work to improve my weaknesses.......to improve my volley I carried out a skill development programme.......I practised the backhand volley close to net......my partner fed me

Physical Education
Higher 2007 (cont)

7. (b) continued

the ball by throwing it to the backhand for me to volley.......gradually the speed and distance was increased .....eventually a feeder would do it from the back of the court........it went from little pressure to more difficulty........eventually to full speed........I would then aim for targets on the court......... then two feeders would drive the ball alternately to forehand and backhand and I had to volley each time ...... I then tried to make it as close to a game as possible by serving to my partner who had to return the serve to my backhand side and I had to volley the ball ....

To improve my second serve I had to aim for targets in the service box ......they were near end of the box so my length of service was deeper ....this would make it a little more difficult for my opponent to return......

This also helped to vary the direction of serve to my opponent......I also tried to learn to serve using top spin .....this would give me some variation on my serve.

(c) When addressing your weaknesses you will have monitored your progress. Explain why this process is important.

Your answer must show knowledge as to why monitoring is important.

Monitoring is important as it provides information on your progress......it allowed me to judge whether my training programme was effective.......it provides me with valuable feedback.....it tells me whether the training was at the correct intensity........it tells me whether improvements were made in the areas I was targeting.......I can take data and compare my performance to previous results......gives me information on what I may still need to work on.....it can also give me motivation .....I can analyse my training on an ongoing basis.

(d) Structures, Strategies or Compositions are based on a number of key principles/fundamentals. For example:
- **Speed in attack**
- **Width/depth/mobility**
- **Using repetition, variation and contrast**
- **The importance of creativity**

Choose two, either from your course or from the list above and explain their importance when applying the Structure, Strategy or Composition. Your answer must show critical thinking as to the importance of each selected principle/fundamental selected when applying your Structure, Strategy or Composition.

For example the importance of creativity. When applying my strategy it is important to be creative.....you need to create a variety of options in response to the changing circumstances in a game......otherwise your opponent will know exactly what you are going to do........they will be prepared and will be able to respond in a particular way.........in tennis in a game it is about ball

7. (d) continued

placement...the position of my opponent and the space available.........doing the unexpected creates an element of surprise ....catching my opponent off guard .....this could be playing a drop volley at net rather than a normal drive......being creative also leads to me being unpredictable ......for example taking the pace off the ball when I serve or serving to my opponent's backhand........this can upset your opponent ......being creative adds flair to your game......can create winners from a difficult position........can win you points.....I could do this also by disguising a shot or direction of the ball......try to wrong foot my opponent........play a drop shot instead of a smash at net when my opponent is at the back of the court.....play a heavy top spin on my second serve.....being creative can also provide different options ....leading to mistakes from my opponent.

The second principle is tempo /speed in play. When applying my Strategy tempo/speed is important.........I need to vary the speed depending on the circumstances to be effective........my service could be delivered at a fast pace or slower for tactical reasons......it could depend on the position my opponent stands to receive the serve ....or where they are when they return the ball....if they are at the back of the court I am more likely to take the pace off the ball.....if I find my opponent is good at passing me as I am at the net after my serve I might stay back.........try to play from baseline and hit the ball with pace from side to side......I could also introduce variation in tempo of my Strategy by varying the depth, pace and using spin or slice in my serve to give me time to get into net.......I want to be able to control each rally so the speed and tempo is important........varying the speed /tempo I play will not allow my opponent to get into a rhythm and dictate play.....will also make my opponent think about each shot ...hopefully lead to mistakes being made.

8. Choose an activity

(a) Describe, in detail, a Structure, Strategy or Composition you have used.

The Strategy I am going to use is half court man to man defence in basketball. The Strategy involves me marking an opponent during a game and as soon as they come into my half of the court it is my role to try and prevent them from scoring a basket or receiving the ball or force them into making mistakes. Each member of my team is responsible for a member of the opposition so each player is marked closely. When playing man to man there are three key positions. These are ball, help and deny. When I am playing "ball" I am defending the player with the ball and I want to try and prevent him/her from making a decisive pass to a team mate or dribbling passed me or shooting. Each player has these three options available and I want to try and prevent all three and force a mistake or get my team a turnover. In "help" it means one of my team mates have lost their player who they were marking, if possible I can help out by moving to try and put pressure and mark their player

8. (a) continued

as this player would have no marker and could be a threat to our team. Finally if I am playing "deny" I am usually one pass away from the player who has the ball in the opposition and it is my job to prevent my player from gaining a pass from that player.

In terms of individual defence I want my body to be low, knees bent, feet shoulder width apart, weight on the balls of my feet, one foot in front of the other so I can shuffle step to change direction and one hand out in front so I can knock the ball away from my opponent. I want to stay between my opponent and the ball and basket and always want to be able to see my opponent as well as the ball.

(b) Discuss some of the problems that either you or your team/group experienced when applying this Structure, Strategy or Composition.

As a team we found that we were poor at communicating. Too often when a player lost the player they were marking they failed to shout for "help" and by that stage the player was often free and punished us as a team by scoring a basket. As a team we were poor generally at "help" defence as too often we were ball watching and concentrating so much on our own player that we forgot we needed to work as a team. This meant on many occasions as soon as a player lost the player they were marking none of our team were in a position to help them often leaving them an easy lay up to score.

Also the opposition had one player who was difficult to stop and was a miss match with the player from our team who was meant to be marking him. This opposition player was very effective at driving to the basket and scoring lay ups and was also effective at scoring close in to the basket. Most of the time the player marking him found it very difficult to prevent him from dribbling past him and get into space and either score or create an opportunity for another team mate.

Finally as individuals our own defence was poor as often we were quite upright in defense rather than being low and the opposition were able to get passed us quickly by dribbling as we did not have the ability to stay with them. Quite often we picked up fouls by lazy defending.

(c) With reference to the problems you experienced in part (b), discuss the decisions you took to develop and improve your performance.

To develop and improve our communication and help defence we did a drill called the "shell" defence drill. In this drill we started with 3v3 with three players marking three of the opposition players in our court. The opposition could pass the ball amongst them without any pressure. As defenders we had to play either ball, help or deny depending on where the ball was in the opposition. If you were playing "help" you were more than one pass away from the person with the ball. Every time the ball was passed we stopped and shouted out what position we were adopting. This was done passively and allowed us to communicate as a team and be quite clear when and how to play "help" defence. Eventually we increased this to 4v4 and then 5v5 to make sure each person

8. (c) continued

could improve their help defence as well as improving our communication skills. We then did the same drill again but this time we played it as a half court game to put our practice back into the pressure situation. To improve the problem we had with the good player from the opposition we decided to double team him whenever he received the ball. This was to be carried out by the nearest player to him. Whenever this player received a pass the nearest player from our team would go and mark him as well as the player designated to mark him. This would mean he was being marked by two players and would restrict his options and cut down the space available to him. This would hopefully put pressure on him and either force a mistake or make him pass the ball and keep him away from the basket.

Finally to improve our individual defence we carried out a drill where the whole class had to adopt a defensive position and you had to stay in this position and follow the teacher or a class mate who was out in front of everybody pointing which direction to go. Then we practised this with a classmate who had a ball and you had to say between your opponent and the ball up and down the court from baseline to baseline where we would change position.

(d) Explain how you evaluated any improvements that were made in your performance in the chosen Structure, Strategy or Composition.

To evaluate the improvements in our performance we videoed a whole game against a team we had played previously. In conjunction with the video we used a game analysis sheet to look at the statistics from the game. On our game analysis sheet we had criteria based on our man/man features including how many times we forced errors, how many times we were able to deny passes being made and especially how many times we managed to help out in defense if a player had lost the player they were marking. We were then able to make a comparison against the first set of results we had taken in our initial information gathering. This would give us an indication whether we had improved as a team and whether our training programme had been successful and most importantly whether the change to double teaming their best player had been effective. For my individual defence I had a criteria checklist consisting of all the features of defense on it and this time I got one of my classmates to tick every time I did any of the criteria well and to cross if it was done badly. Again I compared this to my first checklist to see if I had actually improved.

Physical Education
Higher 2008

AREA 1: PERFORMANCE APPRECIATION

1. **Choose an activity.**

   (a) **Describe in detail your personal performance in relation to two of the performance qualities listed below.**
   - **Technical**
   - **Physical**
   - **Personal**
   - **Special**

   Your answer must demonstrate related knowledge and understanding about how you performed in relation to 2 out of the 4 qualities selected. You should provide specific details with evidence of analytical thinking in relation to your specific strengths and weaknesses.

   For example, the technical qualities I have as a defender in hockey relate to my ball control, dribbling and accurate passes. I believe I am effective and I am consistent on both sides of the field.. and this helps… etc. However I believe my ability to deny space, time and options when in 1v1 situations could be better, I often fail to block space from my opponent and so they get away from me too easily…etc… hockey is physically demanding and fortunately I have high levels of CRE this helps me to…etc

   You should include as much detail as possible.
   If you include **Technical** qualities you may consider some or all of the following points
   - wide repertoire of skills
   - consistent selection and application of skills
   - accurate with high success rate
   - proficient in both attack/defence (if referring to a team game)
   - skilful on both sides e.g. forehand/backhand

   If you select **Physical** qualities you may consider some or all of the following points - i.e some or more of the 6 aspects of fitness
   - strength
   - speed/speed endurance
   - muscular endurance
   - cardio- respiratory endurance
   - flexibility
   - power

   If you select **Personal** qualities you may consider some or all of the following points
   - competitive
   - control of temper/emotions
   - motivated
   - determined
   - focused
   - good leader

   If you select **Special** qualities you may consider some or all of the following points
   - select and apply skills with flair
   - can fake intent
   - create opportunities/space/time
   - disguise placement
   - ability to use both sides of the body skilfully
   - improvise when under pressure

1. (b) **Select one of the qualities highlighted in Part (a). Describe in detail how you gathered information about this quality during your performance when developing your own performance.**

   Your answer **must** include logical and analytical thinking to demonstrate your understanding about the most relevant methods of collecting data/information available. For example, you may have used different methods of analysis which are relevant to general and or focused data. The methods selected may include qualitative or quantitative detail in relation to a selected skill or technique/fitness; general or specific factors and will also reference the validity and reliability issues. In your description of the data/information sources relevant details of associated criteria should be included to reflect the qualities you have selected.
   Examples may include one or more related methods.
   - Movement Analysis (Observation checklist, Match Analysis sheet)
   - Preparation/Action/Recovery: Mechanical Analysis of force, levers, propulsion etc
   - Consideration of Quality: reflecting on whether your skill or technique was controlled/fluent, or fast/slow
   - Video - Comparison of your performance with that of a model performer. The video allows playback, freeze frame.
   - Questionnaire: Questions should be relevant to and have to direct response of done well; needs improvement or grade of 1-5 etc.

   (c) **Why is it important to use appropriate models of performance when developing your own performance?**

   This question is testing your acquired knowledge and understanding about the benefits that model performers can bring to your developmental process. Your response must be detailed and demonstrate critical thinking by offering good examples to support your answer.
   You should consider some of the following important features in your explanation:
   - Identifies your strengths and weaknesses
   - Increases your confidence, motivation
   - Provides you with various types of feedback; qualitative, quantitive, diagnostic etc.
   - Provides you with challenge in practice/competition
   - Provides you with accurate feeds continuously
   - Can inspire you to achieve higher levels of achievement
   - Enables you to plan practice/targets appropriately
   - Enables you to copy ideas

   For example, model performers make my development a faster process for example, I was inspired by them and wanted to be as good as they were… When perfecting my flick pass I got feedback from them and they provided me with 1v1 challenge… I was really motivated by this level of direct competition and used this as a form of target setting; this made me determined to do better… . as I became more skilful I gained in confidence and felt that I could take on more than one opponent…etc

1. (d) **Discuss the importance of goal setting when planning your performance development. Give specific examples of the goals you set.**

This question is testing your acquired knowledge. Your answer must demonstrate related KU and critical thinking in relation to the importance of goal setting. A link to stages of learning, skill complexity, principles of practice may feature in the detail of your answer as your knowledge of these facts will help you set realistic and achievable goals. For example, goals set will help you to

- achieve success developing/applying simple to more complex skills
- set short/long term training targets
- reach personal achievement
- reflect success/monitor improvements
- judge training benefits
- remain motivated/determined/committed
- make future goals

As you develop your answer you must give specific examples of using some of the above. For example, my personal target was to reduce my average score of 6 for a PAR 4 hole. I practised more at the driving range to help me get my drive further up the fairway... etc .. this in turn would let me aim better and also reduce my handicap.

2. **Choose an activity.**

(a) **Explain what you understand about mental factors which affect performance.**

I know that mental factors can have either a positive or a negative effect on performance. I have learned that it is much better to have a positive attitude and control emotions and mental state as this gives the performer the edge and helps them produce an effective performance. Having learned about the different mental factors I know that there 2 main types of anxiety, cognitive and somatic. I have learned that cognitive anxiety can lead to negative thoughts or lack of self confidence; mainly prior to competition. This in turn upsets focus and concentration and mistakes are made. Somatic anxiety is when the body responds by over worrying about situations. This causes the body to react with a physiological response such as sweaty palms, butterflies in stomach, thirst etc. As a result when the body is under stress things like timing, execution of skills, making decisions, taking challenges are handled badly.

Everyone handles pressure and stress in different ways, this depends on people's personality traits. I now know that people react differently to external and internal factors. Performers can learn to deal with these pressures, for example an ability to shut out external factors such as the crowd shouting will enable players to play better. Managing emotions helps performers to be determined and controlled in competitive situations especially when there is a lot at stake. At these times although the performer can be quite aggressive for example, going in for a tackle, the sheer determination and self confidence ensures that a penalty is not given away. Dealing with pressure positively can help the performer display a confident and relaxed manner.

(b) **Select a mental factor that had a negative effect on your performance. What method(s) did you use to overcome this difficulty? Why was the method(s) appropriate?**

During the course of any game players will make mistakes, as a central defender it is crucial that I read play and be aware of the positioning of my opponents. A poor pass back to my goalkeeper almost caused a goal. Instead of forgetting about it I let it get to me. I hate letting my teammates down and worried more about what they might say rather than refocusing and concentrating. I started to get panicky and have negative thoughts in 1v1 challenges I tried to compensate and went in too heavy; I was in danger of being carded. Losing control of my emotions upset my decision making and I started to make more unforced errors. This was early in the game and I knew I had to do something about it if I were to help my teammates and stay on the park. When the ball was up field I used 'self talk' and repeated in my head buzz words to keep me calmer and more focused on my job. It also helped to get shouted at by my teammates, I responded positively to their criticisms and took a few seconds to regroup and think before tackling. I found this improved my judgment which in turn raised my confidence. At half time, our team talk helped and gave me the time to channel my energies to more positive thinking. Self talk is so appropriate as it only takes seconds to complete and helps self determination. Another good thing about 'self talk' is that it can happen simultaneously to the decisions I make for example, as I decide to slide tackle I can talk to myself at the same time to give me that edge, as I close down on the opposition forward I can hear myself say 'mine' or 'Ian's' as I slide my foot in to push the ball clear. Using these buzz words kept me more focused and improved the consistency in my play.

(c) **Select a weakness within your whole performance. Discuss how you planned and managed a programme.**

From my knowledge of training I planned an 8-week training programme to improve my defensive tackling. I felt that the duration of 8 weeks would be a sufficient enough time to see improvements. I knew to consider specificity and thought about the different training methods and different benefits that each had. I decided on a conditioning training programme which included a series of repetition and game-related pressure drills. I think a conditioning approach is more fun and it also let me develop both my skill-related fitness and mental aspects of my performance at the same time. I also found this more motivating as I enjoy the competition and working with my team mates. Football is a fast-paced game and relies on a team effort so it was essential that I practised under similar game conditions. I have to link with my other defenders and read the play to head off the danger, split second timing is crucial. Game drills helped me to adapt quickly to the unexpected. At the same time I knew that I would need to do something about my temper and it was suggested that I used 'self talk' to improve this. I was quite sceptical in the beginning

Physical Education
Higher 2008 (cont.)

2. (c) continued

because it sounded a stupid thing to do. However the regime of deep breathing, focused thoughts and repeating key words in my head such as "Mine, good job, Keep calm- don't say anything - no facial expressions - walk away" forced me to concentrate on the timing of my tackle. Before training I completed these talk phrases 10-15 times and then went onto the field to complete my ball work sessions.

In each of my drills I made sure I worked under pressure; this improved my anticipation to cover space, reduce time and options for my opponent and made me more alert to move earlier to intercept or slide tackle. Firstly I worked on 1v1 possession and tackle drills to 2v4 overload possession in boxed areas. As these drills were performed at 100% intensity contact was inevitable so I learned to control my temper better. For example, even when I was pushed off the ball instead of reacting back or 'giving up' I took a deep breath mark and remained focused to get up and chase back.

The pressure drills of 'give and go' and 'box' practice were completed for different durations with little rest periods, targets were constantly being changed to make sure I reacted to more than one cue at a time, for example, players were cutting into space sometimes 'open' sometimes 'marked', I was forced to consider options and make appropriate decisions and take out the danger man. After 20 minutes of drill practice repetition plays of set pieces such as free kicks and throw-ins were worked on for another 20 minutes. This again forced me to practise my reaction time and anticipation in relation to the ball, the immediate situation and positioning of my team mates and the opposition. This helped sharpen my reaction speed and helped me to make better decisions. These plays were repeated to train me to respond to the 'unexpected' situations and not retaliate or get upset if things did not go according to plan.

I made sure I varied the order of the drills to avoid prediction. As my performance improved I set new targets. I knew to plan around match commitments as some weeks we had mid-week games as well as at the weekend. Having said that I usually play kick around most nights for fun.

Here is how some of my drills were organised.

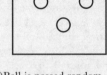

F throws ball to circle, partner and I run forward and challenge for possession.

a)Ball is passed random order between 4 players. Other 2 chase to close down Intercept. b) Same but players move.

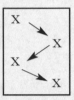

Players at X pass on diagonal D at random slides into challenge. NOTE the tackle is sometimes forward sometimes behind

(d) Explain why it important to review the effectiveness of your programme of improvement.

Not only did the review process ensure I got the best out of each practice session during my training period it was really motivating and kept me on track and determined to succeed. Also when my training was completely finished I knew that it was very important to evaluate whether I was now better than I was before otherwise what was the point. At the start of my training I set targets of the improvements I wanted to achieve. Reviewing my results gave me concrete feedback as I compared my first results and statistics to my last. It was also important for me to look at both my practice and game statistics because this would give me the full picture. Talking to my coach was also important as it backed up my own feelings and helped me to evaluate whether my training programme was pitched at the right level for me, in other words was it specific. I asked myself the following types of questions i.e. had I selected the right type of training? ... had I made right progressions?. .. would I have been better to have included more variation.. was I consistent ...etc...? At the end I was also able to judge whether to continue my training or address other weaknesses that I had. It also gave me confidence to offer advice to others about what worked for me which may give them ideas to include in their training.

AREA 2: PREPARATION OF THE BODY

3. Choose an activity:

   (a) **Describe the physical, skill related and mental fitness requirements for effective performance within your activity.**

   The activity I have chosen is swimming. In swimming cardio respiratory endurance is important. Cardio-respiratory endurance is the ability for the body to work for relatively long periods of time without becoming overtired. When performing in the 100 metres front crawl it is important that the heart and lungs work together to supply the working muscles with oxygen. It is important to have a high level of CRE so I can work longer and harder, especially my arm and leg muscles which help my propulsion. An effective stroke can lead to a faster time overall. Poor CRE will lead to stroke deterioration and a slower time. It is important that I can maintain my technique and breathing for as long as possible before I become tired. A high level of CRE will delay this process. It will also allow me to recover more quickly after the event.
   Strength is also important as I am continuously working the muscles of the arm to generate propulsion to pull the body through the water. Strength is also important to push off the blocks at the start of a race.

   In terms of skill related fitness, coordination is important. This is the ability to work different parts of the body at the same time. In front crawl for example as one arm is pulling the opposite leg should be kicking downwards. Working legs and arms together help me produce the most efficient and effective stroke. Co-ordination is also important in breathing and helps reduce rotation and maintain a streamline position. The longer I can keep swimming with good technique through timing and co-ordination the more effective my stroke will be and hopefully get me a quicker time. I also need good reaction time so as soon as the gun or hooter goes I can push off the blocks and enter the water quickly and efficiently.

   In swimming I require good concentration on things like stroke count to maintain a steady pace and keep my split times consistent. I also need concentration to keep my breathing steady and to achieve an effective turn at the end of each length and in the final swim to the finish. Managing my emotions is important when I am competing. I need to focus on what I am doing and be positive throughout a race and not let myself become anxious or distracted. By being focused I can be in the correct frame of mind to perform well. I need to know what I am going to do in the race and forget about my opponents and spectators watching me. By being properly focused I will not suffer from self doubt and will be ready to compete.

3. (b) **From the fitness requirements described in Part (a) select one aspect. Explain how you gathered information about it within the activity.**

   I have selected CRE which is an aspect of physical fitness. To gather information about it I did the T5 swim test. This is a recognised test which you can do within the activity. The object was to swim front crawl for 5 minutes at an even pace. I was part of a group of four. Each person had a particular job to do: swimming, timing, counting or recording data. We changed each time one person had completed the swim until all of us had swum. The data was collected on a recording sheet. We recorded 20 metre split times and took stroke and breath counts The total distance was recorded and divided by the time taken. An even pace confirmed that CRE was being tested. This gave me information on my level of CRE fitness and I was able to identify my strengths and weaknesses. From this information it allowed me to set targets for my training programme. I could also compare times to other classmates and give me an incentive during training to improve my overall time.

   (c) **There are three phases of training:**
   • **Preparation (pre season)**
   • **Competition (during the season)**
   • **Transition (off season)**
   Discuss why your training might differ between each of the phases. Give examples to support your answer.

   In the preparation phase of training I am trying to build up general fitness work and in particular my aerobic endurance. I could do this by running long/slow distance runs twice per week to start with then gradually increasing this as I get nearer the competition phase. I could also do work like circuit training or particular drills. This means that I am increasing the intensity as I near this phase. The fitness work which I am doing will remain specific to the demands of my event. I would also work on the skills which I require for my activity. Whereas in the competition phase my fitness needs to be maintained. I would be looking to do quality training. In this phase I will have reached a particular level of fitness and will look to rely on the benefits I have gained from pre season. I would also work on specific aspects of fitness that I require for competition. In swimming I could be working on aspects of fitness for example strength and speed endurance. I could work on a strength training programme by doing weights. In this phase I would swim in quite a few races and I would like to peak for these races so my training may increase in intensity for a while and then taper down before the competition. This tapering down allows my body to recover. Here I would decrease the frequency, duration and intensity of each session.The difference in the final phase is that my body is now recovering after competitions and needs to recover. I would cut the training down in order to achieve this. However I would try to maintain a general and reasonable level of fitness. I could take part in other activities for example I could do some cycling or golf or tennis. I would also cut down on the amount of time that I spend on training.

Physical Education
Higher 2008 (cont.)

3. (d) Describe one method of training you used to develop your fitness. Explain why the method was appropriate.

The method of training I used was interval training. This method of training involved me working on periods of high intensity swimming trying to improve my CRE alternating with periods of rest. This work, along with me resting in between, allowed me to train for longer periods of time and therefore allowed me to gain greater benefits from my training. I started off with a warm up then did some stroke/technique work. I then did my main set which was 6x50 metre swim followed by a minute's rest between each set. I then did a sub set of 6x50 metre swim with 45 seconds recovery between each set and then a warm down to finish. Interval training is based on the principle of overload and can develop both aerobic and anaerobic fitness. When I am using interval training the hard work I am doing will ensure that my fitness level is progressing. It is also appropriate as I can vary the time or distance of each period of exercise or the amount of intensity I put in to each exercise or the recovery time or number of sets in each session therefore making it varied and enjoyable. Finally it is also appropriate as I can do this training within the swimming pool.

4. (a) Describe in detail a situation where your level of fitness :
   (i) was a strength to your performance
   (ii) was a weakness to your performance
   (You may wish to answer this question through more than one activity)

Your answer should include a description of a situation using a type of fitness or possibly a particular aspect of fitness within a particular type. Relevant KU should be apparent in the answer in relation to the situation identified and the activity selected. The result to performance will be referred to as a result of the strength and weakness identified.

An example could be:
A strength ... in basketball I play as a centre and ...during a game...the opposition team missed a shot...as I had good strength ...I was able ...to use this to block out my opponent and win the rebound ...so gaining possession for my team.

A weakness ... in hockey late in the game...I lost the ball when attacking ...to the player marking me ...I did not have the stamina to chase back...and dispossess them...they went on to set up a goal for their team.

4. (b) With reference to either the strength or weakness identified in part(a) describe in detail one method of training you used to develop your fitness.

Your answer should show relevant KU in relation to the method of training selected.
This could be wide ranging depending on the strength or weakness selected in part (a). The method must be relevant to type or aspect selected as well. Training could be within activity/out with/ activity/circuit/interval training/ fartlek/ relaxation/rehearsal/weight training
For example trying to improve my CRE for hockey ...I used Fartlek training ...I used the hockey pitch...I ran from start point to 25 metre line and back...then to centre and back...then three-quarter pitch and back...and then full pitch...I did this for 20 minutes...mixing my pace between power walking, jogging and sprinting...this was appropriate to demands in hockey...sometimes I used a ball.

(c) Discuss the principles of training you would consider when designing and completing a training programme.

Your answer must show acquired knowledge of the principles of training and also relevant KU as to how the principles were applied.

Most of the following principles should be referred to:
Frequency, duration, overload, adaptation, progressive overload, rest, recovery, over training, reversibility
Your answer should have a description of how they were applied to a training programme. A good answer will also explain and justify why they would apply the principles used.
For example I made sure the training was specific to the weakness I had previously identified... also to the demands of my role ...and the activity...I trained three times per week ...resting every second day...to allow body to recover...I applied overload after 3 weeks ...as I was getting fitter

(d) Explain why it is important to evaluate the effectiveness of your training programme.

Your answer should show relevant KU and show critical thinking about the importance of evaluating their training programme
For example:
I wanted to know whether my training programme had been effective...also whether it had been appropriate ...to what I had hoped to achieve ...it also provided evidence to compare to previous results...that I had taken at the start of the course
Other reasons could be:
enables changes to be made
• promotes motivation
• whether training was at a correct intensity
• whether your targets or goals have or are being achieved
• making sure you are not overworking

AREA 3: SKILLS AND TECHNIQUE

5. (a) Select two of the influential factors listed below.
- **Motivation**
- **Concentration**
- **Feedback**

Explain what you understand about each factor.

This question is testing your acquired knowledge and understanding about two out of three possible influential factors that affect how you learn, develop or apply your skills.

Your depth of response **must** be detailed and demonstrate critical thinking by offering good examples to support your answer. Regardless of whether you are learning how to perform the skill /technique or are applying the skill/technique some of the following points will effect how successful you are.

You should consider some of the following important features in your explanation in relation to **Motivation**:

- Can be classed as internal/external for example, self motivated, encouraged from coach
- Desire to do better/the need to avoid failure
- Ability to put the work in
- Ability to listen to and act upon feedback
- Ability to stick to task especially when things do not go according to plan
- Can be affected by personality traits/anxiety
- Can be linked to goal setting
- Reinforces learning

You should consider some of the following important features in your explanation in relation to **Concentration**:

- Ability to listen to and act upon feedback; especially when learning new skills
- Ability to remain focused for the duration of the task or when applying skills in competitive situations i.e. think about the tennis player's level of concentration - sometimes in the region of 3 hours
- Ability to focus and process information quickly thus allowing adaptation or improvisation to easily occur
- Ability to store information in your memory and build upon previous experiences
- Ability to shut out external factors such as crowd or opponents
- Ability to respond to stimuli and game cue, for example, move to mark the player or go to intercept the ball

You should consider some of the following important features in your explanation in relation to **Feedback**:

- Must be positive and received as quickly as possible after performance to ensure development
- Can be classed as internal/external, for example, kinaesthetic, written, verbal, visual
- Can be linked to knowledge of performance and or results
- Essential for skill development/refinement as it reinforces learning
- Essential for processing information
- Commonly linked to stage of learning. For example, at the cognitive stage greater demand on external feedback

5. (a) continued
- Commonly linked to skill classification. For example, complex and open skills require both internal and external feedback to ensure effective execution and application of skill or technique especially important when skill/technique has many sub routines

Choose an activity and a skill or technique.

(b) Describe the programme of work that you followed to develop this skill or technique.

This question is testing your applied knowledge in respect of a programme of work you have used to address a skill or technique weakness.

Your depth of response must be detailed and demonstrate critical thinking. You must show evidence of how the selected methods of practice featured as important to your programme. This should be relevant to your identified activity/selected S or T/complexity of the task/Stage of Learning etc. For example, as I was addressing the complex skill of heading on goal from corners when playing football … Etc… I made my problem solving drills game like so that I would be challenged and motivated to succeed…I made my practice harder by adding in more defenders…. I got immediate feedback on my performance so that I had improved… I would know once I had reached my target I would use more complex drills such as … to ensure I do not become bored I decided to …etc

(c) Discuss how the principles of effective practice were applied to the programme.

This question is testing your acquired understanding about the principles you need to consider to make practice effective by examining how you applied these principles to your practice programme.

The depth of your answer must be in full detail and exhibit detailed KU about relevant principles. Your responses should reflect that practice methods selected for improvement should be specific to the complexity of skill and relevant to your stage of learning. The acronym S.M.A.R.T.E.R. is useful for this purpose. For example, practice should be specific, measurable, attainable, realistic, time related, exciting and regular. Other relevant knowledge will reference factors such as practice needs to show progression to ensure targets were reached/enabled refinement/remediation/ regression as required, increased motivation, improved confidence, consideration of work rest ratio etc.

(d) Explain how your whole performance was affected on completion of this programme of work.

This question is testing your ability to critically evaluate improvements if any to your performance as a result of following your programme of work.

The depth of response will reflect upon the selected development of skill or technique. You must show critical thinking and offer evaluative comments about improved performance. This must be supported with relevant information about how your whole performance was affected. For example, on completion of my training I could see that I more

Physical Education
Higher 2008 (cont.)

5. (d) continued

consistently scored more goals … The execution of my header was much more directed and had more power… I could now… etc .. I timed my run into the box and connected much much better from crosses played in from the left… I tallied up more hits on target than previously…I was more able to take on body charges from more than one defender when in the air.. etc

6. Choose an activity and a skill or technique.

(a) Select one of the following approaches. Describe how you gathered information about your chosen skill or technique using this approach.
- **Mechanical analysis**
- **Movement analysis**
- **Consideration of quality**

In dance, I decided to gather information about the quality of my solo piece so that I could identify any problems with it and make it more interesting to watch. I used a consideration of quality sheet; this was a self evaluation report after studying a video of my performance. I wanted to look at not only my technical competence in the simple and complex techniques included in my dance but highlight how effectively I moved to the music and how I used variations of tempo, direction and gestures to make my dance highly energetic. As other qualities should be evident in my performance like flair, timing, creativity and choreography design, the consideration of quality sheet was definitely the most appropriate for me to use.

I performed my solo piece several times and had it video recorded. I examined the replay several times before watching it in slow motion it was at this time I completed a self evaluation sheet and assessed the quality of each of my transition moves on a scale of 1 - 4 (1 meaning limited and 4 meaning excellent). To ensure reliability I then watched my performance again and got feedback from my teacher to make sure it was a detailed account.With the transitions that I assessed at a 1; in my case my 'pas de chat'. To make sure I got more detail I used a more focused consideration of quality sheet to analyse specific parts of this movement in more detail. This sheet contained the quality criteria of a model performer. Again my performance was assessed using this criterion. I was then able to compare my performance against the model performer and get valuable feedback on how effectively I transferred my weight, varied the speed and tempo.

I was then able to prioritise my needs and plan a skills improvement programme. I would then be able to use this sheet during my dance sessions and refer to it to see if I was improving.

6. (b) Discuss the results of the information gathered in part a). Make specific reference to how your whole performance was affected.

With reference to the information I had gathered I felt I demonstrated good control and fluency with many specific moves. The tempo of the music has fast and energetic and this dictated to some extent the dynamics and transitions that I included, for example, lots of spinning, slide stepping, single and double pirouettes. My choreographic skills showed that I had good creativity and lots of variation in linking movements to utilise the floor space. I included good gestures with both my hands and head; some of which were sustained and others fast and jerky. I maintained energy to the music tempo to show good interpretation and make my dance look exciting.

To be a good dancer takes hours of practice, even the simple skills take time to master. The more complex ones, like double pirouette, pas de bourree and pas de chat are very complex and demand solid physical training as well as repetitive technique drills. Finally once the skills are mastered in isolation I have to spend hours rehearsing the best possible choreographic composition.

My weakness was my inability to consistently perform the pas de chat. The pas de chat is a dynamic jump in the air. When in the air my legs are back with my feet touching my buttocks and my knees must be apart.

When I perform this I find it hard to get sufficient height off the ground to give me time to bring my feet up quickly behind me. As you can see my knees should be apart when in the air, mine are usually too close together. On landing I must be balanced ready to head/hand gesture before moving into the next sequence of my dance.

Having compared my performance to the model performer I was able to see that this loss of shape and form caused me to look quite clumsy and interrupted the rhythm of my moves. When performing in competition I have different arena to perform in. Sometimes I have an open floor space where the audience is all around me. Sometimes I am on stage where the audience is in front of me. I find that when I perform on stage I make most mistakes in my pas de chat.

6. (c) **Outline the programme of work that you followed to develop your performance in this skill or technique. Explain why this programme of work was appropriate.**

I decided I would need to work on developing the physical aspects of flexibility and power. Flexibility would enable me to stretch my legs wider into position and the power in my legs would help me get more height and so give me more time in the air. I decided to do this in a form of circuit training. The circuit involved me visiting 6 different stations. Each station had specific exercises with different levels of difficulty, for example, in the plyometric jumps I had the option of selecting the bench or box top to jump down from. Similarly in the mini jumps I could vary the height of the hurdles. At the flexibility stations I worked on both dynamic and static stretches concentrating on the abductor and adductor muscles. On my non training days I used repetition sequences of the parts of my dance that needed the most rehearsal.

After a warm up I focused on my flexibility exercises first and moved around 3 stations. At each station I maintained a varied leg split position to stretch the leg muscles required in my pas de chat. I knew to apply principles of training and performed each of these 3 stretches at 100% intensity for 20 - 30 secs. I specifically organised these stretches to address leg positioning and increased range of movement. After 20/30 secs I released the pose, loosening off the muscles before repeating the action. I did this x3 before moving onto the last 3 stations which addressed the power in my legs. One station involved me jumping down from the box top and immediately jumping over the bench, another involved a series of two footed jumps over 6 mini hurdles, with the last station varied hops and jumps in and out of the ladder. I tried to do as many repeats as I could for 1 minute. During rest periods I recorded my score this was an incentive and let me see how hard I was working. It was important to take adequate rest periods to help improve my recovery before moving on to the next station. I repeated the 6 station circuit again x3. To progress I increased the circuit to 3 then to 5 as the weeks went by.

I knew to include high energy repeats of the pas de chat technique during my rehearsal days to make sure I was getting the best out of my physical training.

(d) **Explain why it is important to monitor and review your programme of work.**

I know that it is very important to do both. Monitoring is very, very important as this should be happening at the time. As I trained I always checked on how I was doing via my personal best scores. I found that this kept me motivated and it provided with immediate feedback. I challenged myself during training and noted the things I was doing better and targeted the things I could still improve upon. If I found I was not reaching my targets I adjusted them. For example, if I found that my plyometric drills were too easy then I made them harder. Monitoring also lets me see how I am doing compared to my fellow dancers, for example in the flexibility exercises I was able to see if I was getting as lower in the split position and in my solo repeats if

6. (d) continued

my pas de chat was showing better height and technique display. Monitoring is constant as internally I could feel the improvements and could also feel when I needed to work harder.

Reviewing my performance I did most when I had completed my training programme. This let me compare my first performance to my most current. I would be able to check if the training programme had worked. Had I reached my long term goals? Was I able to perform my pas de chat better not only when practicing but when performing on stage? Was my solo piece more dynamic and exciting to watch? Reviewing my training let me judge whether or not to continue my training on the same aspects or whether to move and address other weaknesses. Reviewing is also necessary as it let me evaluate whether the type of training I used worked and motivated me to select it again.

AREA 4: STRUCTURES AND STRATEGIES

7. **Choose an activity**

(a) **Describe a Structure, Strategy or Composition that you have used. What were your strengths when applying this Structure , Strategy or Composition.**

Your answer must show acquired KU regarding Structure, Strategy or Composition selected and describe the strengths you had when applying it. It may have some detail regarding the aim of it and it is acceptable to possibly make reference to the role you played. The Structure, Strategy or Composition selected must be appropriate for the activity.
For example, we play 3-5-2 in football…three defenders…5 midfield with…2 strikers…my role is wing back in midfield …in attack I need to… provide width close to touchline…make runs into opponents box …deliver quality crosses into box…in defence delay attacks..
My strengths were…I was good at providing width for my team in defence and attack…I was good at tackling …winning the ball in midfield… good at covering for team mates …I also had good decision making skills when to attack …good at reading the game

(b) **Discuss how you planned your performance to make best use of your strength(s) when performing in this Structure, Strategy or Composition.**

Your answer must demonstrate applied KU of how you planned to make best use of the strengths you had when performing. Critical thinking must be shown. For example:
against a team we had played before I knew they played 4-3-3…their two full backs liked to act as wingers when attacking …and get up pitch to support midfield…my job was to track the player on my side… and prevent him doing this…as a good tackler I often won the ball and started an attack…also exploit space as full back was out of position.

Physical Education
Higher 2008 (cont.)

7. (b) continued

Various factors may be shown in answers. These could include:

- Use particular players in particular roles
- Type of opposition
- Attack/defence being applied by team or opposition
- Strengths of particular players
- Time restrictions
- Knowledge of opponents from previous games

(c) Describe your weakness(es) when applying this Structure, Strategy or Composition. Discuss the effect this had on your performance.

You must be able to describe your weakness(es) when applying this Structure, Strategy or Composition and demonstrate detailed discussion on the effect on performance. Critical thinking must be shown in your answer.

Weakness(es) may be from a team or an individual. For example:

In my role as a wingback...the quality of the final ball into the box was poor...at the end of a run taking me beyond the defence...my decision making was poor as to the type of ball into the box...I often hurried the cross ...if I was under pressure...and it went over the heads of our attackers as it was too hard ...or it went out of play ...or straight to the goalkeeper or opposing defenders who cleared the ball...I failed to create the opportunities for the forwards...also as the game progressed I was unable to get up and down the park due to poor CRE...I became less effective in my role...if I was caught up field I could not get back ...to defend ...and help out...or make challenges. I needed to pace myself better during the game

(d) Explain what you did to reduce the effect of the weakness(es) identified.

Your answer must demonstrate critical thinking and decision making to explain how the effect of the weakness(es) were reduced.

The responses will be dependent on the choice of Structure, Strategy or Composition selected. The answer could include a description of the programme of work to improve weakness but must be relevant. For example :

To help make better decisions about final ball...I practised 5 variations...at training I practised all these options ...with my team mates and in particular the 2 strikers...initially with no defenders then with a full defence...as close to match play as possible...by setting definite options in this way I could improve my decision making.

To improve my CRE I ...carried out a training programme ...did fartlek training...this involved long and short running on football pitch...which imitated the movements in an actual game ... I sometimes dribbled the ball ...to half way line ...left it ...then ran back ...then ran to collect it and leave it at 18 yard line ...and so on ...I also decided to work on an alternative strategy ...the striker on my side would come short...receive ball ...pass back to me ...and then sprint down my channel ...I would chip the ball to him to run on to...this would mean I do not have to use up as much energy ...by running up my side all game

8. Choose an activity.

(a) Discuss the factors you would take into consideration when selecting a Structure, Strategy or Composition.

The activity chosen is basketball.

When considering selecting a particular strategy I would take into account first of all the strengths and weaknesses of the opposition that we are playing against. If we had played them previously I would have some idea of what they were like as a team and would know what players were good or who was weak at particular things. This may then allow me to decide upon a particular strategy which could exploit these weaknesses or counteract their strategy. For example if I knew the opposition had good outside shooters when playing basketball I would decide to play half court man to man to nullify this and force them to drive to the basket.

I would also consider the strengths and weaknesses of my own team and in particular certain players who may be able to carry out specialist roles with the activity. For example 'when playing basketball in man/man defence who is my best defender?', 'who could win us turnovers as a team or force most mistakes from the opposition?', 'who is my concern if a player fouls?' and 'do we have a good substitute should they be needed in a game?'

I also would take into account the fitness level of our team and how long we could carry out the strategy before fatigue set in and our play started to deteriorate. The score and time in an actual game are factors to take into account. If we are losing and we are in the last few minutes of a game then we might decide to change or select a strategy which would be effective at this stage of the game and possibly let us win in the final few minutes. Finally the previous results of the opposition if we had played them before will be taken into account. I would know what had happened and how we won or lost the match and that may have an influence on what strategy I might use.

(b) Describe in detail a Structure, Strategy or Composition you have used.

The strategy I have used is the fast break in basketball. This can start after a basket has been scored by the opposition, a rebound from my team, from a change of possession or an end line ball. The object is to try and score a basket as quickly as possible once you receive the ball and catch the opposition before they can set up a good defence. From the rebound the forward out wide in a line opposite our free throw line received an outlet pass from the rebounder. This player would now dribble the ball down the centre of the court towards the opposition key area. The other forward out wide who did not receive the first pass and the person who rebounded the ball would run down the side of the court filling the wide lanes. The player with the ball at the top of the key now has a choice of what to do. They can drive to the basket themselves if it is clear or pass the ball to one of the two players who have filled the outside lanes and the player receiving the ball can drive to the basket and score with a lay up.

8. (c) **Briefly describe a situation where you had to adapt or change the Structure, Strategy or Composition in part (b). Discuss why these changes or adaptations made your performance more effective.**

When we were playing against another school they became familiar with our fast break as we tended to use the same break all the time. They knew exactly what the ball handler was going to do each time they reached the top of the key and as soon as the ball handler made the pass the forward was put under pressure and often was stopped in their drive to the basket causing the break to stop. This prevented us from scoring baskets and we had to try another play. We decided to change the options we could use in the break. The same initial parts of the break were carried out but as soon as the ball carrier reached the half way circle they now passed the ball early to one of the forwards at the side who then dribbled for a few strides and then passed the ball diagonally across the key to the other clear forward who had an easy drive to the basket to score a lay up. This caused an element of surprise and caused the defence to be caught unawares. It also meant as the ball was passed earlier at the half way line there was less time for the defence to get back and allowed our team more time and space to drive to the basket. We also added another option from this break where the forward who received the diagonal pass could fake to drive and reverse the ball back to the ball carrier who had now reached a position just inside the key for a close jump shot to the basket. Again this caused an element of surprise. It now meant that we had various options we could use and the defence could not predict which break we were going to use. This meant that the fast break worked successfully more often and we scored more baskets.

(d) **Having adapted or changed the Structure, Strategy or Composition explain how you would evaluate its effectiveness.**

We evaluated the effectiveness of the adapted strategy by using a video linked to a game analysis sheet. We videoed a game against the same opponents and afterwards used an analysis sheet with all aspects of the changes to the fast break on it. The data which we gathered from this enabled us to see whether the adapted strategy was effective and then we were able to compare this to the data which we had gathered from the original strategy. It gave us useful information as to the effectiveness of the adapted strategy and also allowed us to see which of the options which we could now carry out was the most effective. From the data collected we were also able to identify where the fast break broke down and that gave us information which we could work on in training.